Always Start Your Day with

C.O.F.F.E.E

Energy for your Soul

T. Pearl Joynz

Publishing Information

ISBN Printed Version: 978-1-7352063-0-1

Edited by Annie Jenkinson

Table of Contents

Dedication

For my family and friends, for me, and always for my faith!

This book is dedicated to my grandmother, Annette Marie Jones who gave me my first cup of literal and figurative coffee. I miss you every day! It is also dedicated to my three little ducks, Summer, Autumn, and Asher. May you always have full cups of C.O.F.F.E.E.

The secret things belong to the LORD our God, but the things revealed belong to us and to our children forever, that we may follow all the words of this law.

\-   Deuteronomy 29:29

Introduction

—— ❧ ——

"In Him was life, and that life was the light of all mankind."

\-   John 1: 4

Now, let's all be honest; who doesn't need a little wisdom, energy and light in their life? I'm sure we all do! Well, the good news is that there are so many ways to energize your soul, and this book seeks to point you in the direction of what I consider an eternal source of wisdom and energy. And it all begins with coffee! Really, it does. But maybe not in the way you think.

Let's back-track just a little so I can tell you my story of how I came to write this book, and then I will tell you all about the coffee. Sit yourself down someplace comfortable, take a deep breath and let your inner coffee pot get warm…

Where this all begins is that science teaches us how light itself is a source of energy, described as *pure energy,* something that cannot be stored and is always moving, forever shifting.

Therefore, we know that Jesus Christ, who was described as *the light of the world* is a source of pure energy, His light eradicating darkness and providing great energy for our souls if we allow it.

As people of faith, we harness an energy source provided by our Creator, in the form of the Holy Spirit. We seek light as a natural deterrent to the darkness existing in our world, and seek energy to serve Him in spirit and in truth. We seek the opportunities He provides to introduce others to the joy existing in energetically serving Him.

And we can reach the energy and spirit of our Creator, and all his light and joy by beginning every day with coffee.

The premise of this book—and its coffee message, one that I love—were passed onto me by my maternal grandmother, who said, "Always start your day with coffee!" In fact, this was the last piece of advice my grandmother provided to me; I feel her love and stamp of approval on every single page.

My grandmother was a vivacious, little woman with a big heart, the heartbeat of our family, someone who set me on my journey of faith. She was loving and kind and never met a stranger, welcoming every soul into her heart and home no matter who they were.

She loved to tell stories, to help others, and always sought out ways that would make everyone's lives better. But most of all, I remember her generosity; she never held anything back from anyone. If she saw that you were hurting, it became her personal mission to assist and I am so grateful I had a front-row seat to witness how she devoted her energy to this.

Figure 1: The author with her grandmother.

A few years before she passed, I remember her reminiscing about her life, telling me that she believed she had missed her calling of becoming a nurse.

She revealed, "if I could do it all over again, I would have pursued nursing as my chosen career."

I laughed and reminded her that she had been a nurse in her own right, providing natural cures and words of encouragement to anyone who would listen. In this regard, who knows, maybe she had helped so many more than she could have done as a medical nurse, since healing the mind is possibly even more valuable than healing the body.

She healed so many of us in the immediate family and local community with her personal touch, prayers and recommendations. We both laughed together, and she said, "Well, I guess you are right." She then went on to explain how proud she was of me for joining the military and of the woman I had become. She never withheld her praise or thankfulness.

When she died in 2005, it was as if a light went out in my soul. Even though I had said my goodbyes, her illness was sudden and I was not prepared for one of my life's compasses to be taken away. I was in Hawaii at the time and my mother recommended that I come home immediately if I could, so I did and within a few days, my grandmother departed this earth, leaving behind a giant hole in my heart.

And perhaps you won't be able to imagine that it has taken me fifteen years to complete this book, due to the loss of her from my life and also because I was still trying to understand quite what she had meant by always starting your day with coffee! I did not want to misunderstand or misrepresent her words; it was only over the years that all the meanings came to me, becoming clearer and clearer, until it was as if I held onto a beacon of light that no longer wanted to be entrapped; it needed freeing from my hands and letting out into the world, our Creator's world, so that you too could bathe in it. In writing this book, I was setting her light free to do its work.

Originally, I had not known what she meant, and it was difficult to think about her without being overwhelmed with sorrow. Even as I write this introduction today, it is through tears, because there have been so many moments I wish she had been here to see.

The birth of my two younger children whom she would have adored are at the top of my list, but I know she is on the balcony of Heaven cheering us on. I know she is there.

My grandmother died when my oldest daughter was five, yet she always talked about my son as if he was following close behind! She would say, "you just wait until the boy gets here."

Well, he did not arrive until 2013, but because of my grandmother's words, I was waiting for him; her unwavering foreshadowing of him helped me survive four miscarriages while I continued to believe her premonition and God's voice telling me the same.

My middle daughter is like my grandmother in so many ways, and I often joke that raising her is akin to raising my grandmother, since she is what many refer to as an old soul. She is frequently asking me can she have a cup of coffee and every time she does, I smile and think of my grandmother and of how they would have been the best of friends.

A couple of years ago, I wrote my first book, entitled, "*The Shattering*". The process was different because it poured out of me easily. In that instance, writing was a coping mechanism from the chaos I was dealing with personally and professionally.

Thinking again about *this* book, however—C.O.F.F.E.E—I felt some guilt as I knew this should have been my first one, being the first book idea that I believed came to me from God. So, I prayed to God for assistance, since I could no longer ask my grandmother what she had meant, yet I knew I was destined to write it. God was so gracious to me and through the Holy Spirit, He filled in the blanks with insight and revelations.

I quickly realized this could benefit so many other people and it began to make sense that sharing it would be a beautiful memorial to my grandmother and to Jesus Christ, who allowed her to share it with me. Living in Christ has given my life meaning and purpose, and if I had written it all those years ago, it would surely have been incomplete. I did not have enough life under my belt to properly understand the richness of her assertion. I also could not have purposed my energy properly toward this project as I ran toward other personal undertakings such as building a career, finishing a doctoral degree in Education, raising children, and sustaining a strained marriage.

Today, I have a better understanding of the message she was trying to tell me, and I am better able to offer it to you. I have grown in godly wisdom through experiences and trials; many of the devotions and revelations were written in an intense season of personal pain and suffering.

It was a devastating and lonely time, yet God was so close I could see Him in every moment, and I could feel His love through every person He provided to assist me during those dark days. I am also convinced that the timing for this book was not right until this very moment. God inspires us daily, but we must trust His timing, because He knows all and sees all. He never once condemned me for my lack of writing this book despite entrusting the task to me, but He knew I kept it in the forefront of my mind and when the time was right, he gave me both the green light and the wisdom and energy to complete it.

Now, I had what I needed, and it began to fall into place.

Our world needs healing, inspiration and positive energy. There is no mistake I am releasing this book in 2020, a year that has been a whirlwind of emotions, decay, and lack globally. A global pandemic has ensued thanks to the novel coronavirus pandemic and its wretched disease, Covid-19. Millions of people have been infected and so many have died. Stay-at-home orders have been issued, resulting in panic, political protests, and poverty.

Churches, which used to be the staple of the community, have been sidelined and shut down as part of the effort to "flatten the curve" of the spread of the virus. Several pastors have died from it and some have been fined and/or arrested for their refusal to stop holding services. But just as there is no way to stop the virus yet, so too is there is no way to stop God spreading his word and his work! Churches have become creative in their endeavors.

Instead of in-person services, virtual services are now being offered to keep the Body of Christ connected. Church, as we have known it during our lifetime, may never be the same again—who knows? But this is not a cause for alarm, so do not be afraid of change here, because *we are the church* and as long as we have breath in our bodies, the doors of the church are well and truly open!

Many spiritual leaders have also noted that the modern-day church does not remotely resemble the ministry of Jesus Christ, who never confined ministry to an edifice. As such, are we now praising God in a manner more aligned to how our Lord's ministry began?

It is at least worth thinking about, rather that than getting depressed because "things have changed."

We have a unique opportunity to reconnect to God and to determine what His plan is for our individual lives and the model for the modern-day collective church, once this is over.

It will only be the arrogant who do not stop to ask God for an assessment or what His desires are during this time. I find this fascinating, as I have long been complaining about the busy, rapid life we all live. But I, too, felt the initial angst caused by being quarantined and having my daily life disrupted.

I do not believe God sent this virus, but I do believe He allowed it, because to deny that is to deny his sovereignty. I am fully convinced He is going to use this for our spiritual good. I am concerned, however, that many believe His good is only tied to finances and prosperity instead of our faith.

I continue to hear people chide, "life is never going to be the same." Well, that's true; maybe it won't be. Maybe it will become better.

I find hope in this statement of change, and am looking forward to God's correction, direction, and plan for my future.

And—not least since you still do not know about the coffee—let's find out what this is all about and how coffee can help you meet the change head on, with positivity and imbued by God's spirit.

How to Use This Book

—————— ⌇ ——————

"In Him we live and move and have our being. As some of your own poets have said, We are His offspring."

-   Acts, 17:28

This book should be used to enhance and accompany your increasing knowledge of the Holy Bible. It is not intended to be a replacement. You will find many scriptures as I share various stories and concepts, but it is my hope this will encourage you to seek for yourself the passages out in their full context.

So, this finally brings me to let you in on the secret of the coffee!

C.O.F.F.E.E is a personal anagram I developed to provide spiritual clarity for the advice I received. There are six main sections (**C**onfidence, **O**bedience, **F**ervent Prayer, **F**ruit of the Spirit, **E**arnest Expectation, and **E**verlasting Life) provided to energize your soul, based upon my coffee acronym. Positive energy may be obtained from every area listed above.

"Energize" is defined as "giving vitality and enthusiasm to", exactly what every believer should strive to obtain, and the good news is that God has already provided it in the form of His Word, God's Holy Word found in the pages of the Bible.

This is an often untapped power source.

The process of writing this book reminded me of the slow-brewed coffee pot of my childhood. Its aroma filled the room before we ever got to take a sip from it, but according to my grandmother, it was always worth the wait! We would bake and talk while the coffee would brew, and she laughed enough to make her whole body shake, her smile and laughter both infectious. Her positive energy never seemed to end.

In each main section of this book, there will be introductory insights to enhance your understanding of the topic of C.O.F.F.E.E. Next, tips accompany each section as recommended, practical application of each biblical concept discussed.

Lastly, you will find devotions to support to the C.O.F.F.E.E concept and encourage you to think more broadly about it. These are equivalent to your breakfast, lunch, and dinner cup of coffee, showing you how you can integrate these into your day to receive the sustenance that you need from each.

Take notes, meditate on His word and genuinely read this book with God. Allow Him to show you brand new things and offer you fresh perspectives. Be curious about your future and your purpose.

I hope you savor every drop the Lord provides in the pages below.

May you find lasting peace in what will be revealed within.

Chapter 1:

Confidence

"My soul will make its boast in the LORD; The humble will hear it and rejoice."

-   Psalm 34: 2

Confidence is the feeling or belief that one can rely on someone or something: it means having a firm trust. And confidence is represented by the C in **C.O.F.F.E.E.**

There are many reasons that we should place our confidence in Christ. He has proven himself to be authentic, capable, and trustworthy. In my life, no other entity or person has consistently provided the level of careful attention to my daily needs than He has.

I lived without him for too many years and placed my confidence in other things and people, which was foolish. I have learned through heartache and setbacks that only He will hold me up when I fall, and I can fully rely on his counsel, guidance and wisdom.

2 Corinthians 10:17 says, "but he who boasts is to boast in the LORD."

If this is the case, we must begin to know and believe what God can do, has done, and will do in our lives.

We can place our confidence in Christ because He has a proven track record. If this is an area that you personally struggle with, you will want to search the scriptures expressing how God sees you and what He says about you. He is the creator of mankind and knows his original design better than we do, forming us from the dust and breathing his breath of life into us. The Bible is full of insights of what God wants us to think about ourselves and Him, a guidebook with answers to all our curiosities, longings, and worries.

Seeking His source document provides us with fuel to face each day confidently. I do not have to fear the day or its troubles, because I am confident that I never walk alone when following Christ!

We continuously place our confidence in worldly principles and inventions, yet doubt spiritual precepts. I will again reference the coffee maker to keep with our theme.

When people properly load this appliance with coffee and a filter, they are confident it will produce coffee. They do not have anxiety or concern about it creating soda. Yet, our trust in Christ must be even more steadfast than our trust in modern appliances. Once we have been forgiven of sin, we have been provided a fresh coffee filter and choice coffee beans capable of producing stellar cups of coffee. We should rejoice knowing we can produce numerous flavors if we use His equipment, recipes, and supplies. We should also know we serve a God who continues to provide fresh filters as needed.

Confidence Tip of the Day

Look in the mirror and say, "No matter what happens today, God has a plan, the provision, and a purpose!" Just as you may take several coffee top-ups during a certain period, you may need to repeat this throughout your day.

Confidence Tip of the Month

Seek out and interview an older believer; this can be based on age or years serving God. I highly recommend an elderly saint if possible because many of them enjoy the company and sharing their life experiences. Also, many of us leave this earth without being able to pass on remarkable examples of what God has done through us, to us and for us.

Confidence Tip of the Year

Reflect on the last year by sitting with your calendar open and remembering how many days you were alive, how many breaths you took, how many meals you ate and how many people you encountered.

Write down what was noteworthy (good or bad) and acknowledge that you were never alone. If this year were to be a movie or a book, what would the title be?

Write it down as a memorial and envision what you want the next year's title to reflect.

It's Only a Test

It is a pleasure to share a thought for all believers sitting in God's classroom today.

Life is full of tests, and when taking a test, we all know that preparation is the key to success; the same can be said of your Christian journey in this world. We are required to take several spiritual tests as we seek promotion to the next level in God's Kingdom.

The good news is, we can't fail the final exam, because our teacher is phenomenal, and He grades on a curve (mercy), and He is so smart.

Nevertheless, you mustn't fool yourself into thinking you can study later; you just never know when you will get a pop quiz.

To understand how important the tests are, I am obligated to pass a few study tips on to you as you prepare for your next test:

Using Cliff notes only will more than likely get you a D;

Watching a movie and trying to remember what you saw will probably get you a C;

Listening to the instructor, taking notes for later and studying it will likely get you a B.

However, if you want to score that elusive A in your final exam, READ THE BIBLE!

"Do your best to present yourself to God as one approved, a worker who does not need to be ashamed and who correctly handles the word of truth." **2 Timothy 2:15**

"Blessed is the one who perseveres under trial because, having stood the test, that person will receive the crown of life that the LORD has promised to those who love him." **James 1:12**

"So I turned my mind to understand, to investigate and to search out wisdom and the scheme of things and to understand the stupidity of wickedness and the madness of folly." **Ecclesiastes 7:25**

When I was in high school, I barely cracked open a book and certainly never took one home. I took a lot of shortcuts in studying and graciously still did well, ending up a B student (thank you, Jesus). This does not work in the spiritual classroom God has placed us in.

Here, you must rely on the guidance of the Bible and your instructors to achieve a *passing* score and must study God's words to achieve the *highest* score. Whether you consider yourself scholarly or not, you will find all of the answers in God's book. I have determined in my heart to be on God's Honor Roll. Remember to be *confident*—there's that word again—that God has given you the answers you will require.

Be encouraged in this, since our God is so gracious and merciful, always giving us an open-book test!

Don't Put the Cart before the Horse!

Some time ago, I was driving down the highway and noticed a horse trailer beside me. It was a big one that could fit several horses, and it caught my attention because I consider myself one of God's horses.

Horses are used for transportation, one way of taking our Savior wherever he needs to go. I am honored to give Jesus a ride, and honored to go where he goes. I love the visual in Revelation 19 of the Horse and the Rider, and this is where my new-found love for horses comes from and, in particular, white horses.

Revelation 19:11-13, says, "Now I saw heaven opened, and behold, a white horse. And He who sat on him *was* called Faithful and True, and in righteousness, He judges and makes war. His eyes *were* like a flame of fire, and on His head *were* many crowns. He had a name written that no one knew except Himself. He *was* clothed with a robe dipped in blood, and His name is called The Word of God. And the armies in heaven, clothed in fine linen, white and clean, followed Him on white horses."

As I saw the horse trailer, my mind wondered where the horses were going and where I was heading, for we are always in transit. God has us on a detailed, specific journey that we don't know or have directions to yet. We are figuratively riding in the horse trailer until He takes us out, saddles up, and leads us where He has destined us to go.

I love this because I am learning to enjoy the ride instead of worrying about where I'm headed. My only focus is to follow His lead, slowing down when He tells me to and speeding up when He nudges. I can be *confident* in my Lord's provision!

God's Provision

After passing the trailer, about fifteen miles ahead of me, I saw another truck carrying what appeared to be hay or stubble. It was not in bale, and was already spread out and ready for use. The truck carrying the hay was a commercial truck, not affiliated with the privately owned truck I saw pulling the horse trailer, but nonetheless they needed each other.

At that moment, it dawned on me that God's provision goes before us. Everything we need in this life, He has already provided it ahead of time. So, we need not worry so much about the *what ifs* in life, i.e. what if we get to where we are going and X or Y happens. God has already seen to it. We just have to have faith and let Him provide ahead.

T. D. Jakes once said, "God is not preparing the blessing for you; He is preparing you for the blessing." If both trucks I saw were going to the same destination, then the hay (provision) being carried by the commercial truck (cart) was going to arrive before the consumer (the horse).

Wow….God! You mean all my needs are already met; I just need to keep walking? This is like going away on vacation and not having to pack and carry all the bags. I'm all for that! And this is exactly what the Lord wants to share with you today.

I know you have heard all your life, "don't put the cart before the horse." It appears, though, that this is precisely what God does, so why should we live life so cautiously and so stressed out about not getting what we require? Be confident—that's all.

He has stored up blessings, provision, and grace for you in his Kingdom and on the earth. I believe this, and it was a reaffirmation that day on Interstate 64 West. Those horses didn't have to worry about their next meal because it was already provided and would be ready for them.

What Does the Scripture Say about This?

Isaiah 55:8 - 9 says, "For My thoughts are not your thoughts, Nor are your ways My ways," declares the Lord. For as the heavens are higher than the earth, So are My ways higher than your ways And My thoughts than your thoughts."

Psalms 144:8 declares, "Our barns will be filled with every kind of provision. Our sheep will increase by thousands, by tens of thousands in our fields."

Matthew 6:26 directs us to, "Look at the birds of the air: They do not sow or reap or gather into barns, and yet your Heavenly Father feeds them. Are you not much more valuable than they?"

Scripture provides us with the key to worry-free living

and the truth that God does supply all of our needs in accordance with Philippians 4:19, which encourages us to know, "But my God will supply all your need according to His riches in glory by Christ Jesus."

This is a powerful principle as we continue to walk with the Lord daily. He is a sustainer, provider, and lover of His children. He puts the cart before the horse, and whatever you need today, it is already prepared for you.

Beauty is All around us and in Us

Before you were born, the Lord knew your needs and your purpose because he hand-designed you. You were custom ordered, a work of art by a Master Craftsman, and set on display for the entire world to see. You are God's masterpiece.

As I marveled at the beautiful trees I passed on I-64, I saw a beautiful tree clothed in bright yellow leaves, and said, "That is so beautiful." Deep in my spirit, I felt the Lord say, "Not as beautiful as you are to me."

The Lord was confident in that, wasn't He?

See how self-assuredly he said it.

It gave me pause to reflect upon how the Lord sees me and to know that He who created the most beautiful wonders our eyes will ever examine, continues to see the beauty in each of His children.

Whoa, Horsey!

This message I share with you can be summed up in Ephesians 2:10, "For we are God's handiwork, created in Christ Jesus to do good works, which God prepared in advance for us to do."

Did you notice the "preparation" principle? This is by God's design, so we would have no need to worry, knowing he has prepared the good works and the ability for us to complete them. You are the horse; you are not responsible for the cart. God is.

I agree we should not put the cart before the horse, because we don't have any business messing with the cart in the first place. The cart is God's work.

The cart is none of your concern, so stop trying to figure out where it is, stop trying to purchase one, and rest in the knowledge that in due season, you will catch up to it.

It will be at the right spot at the right time, waiting there for you! Your focus should only reside in *preparation of the horse in anticipation of the rider* because God is the source for whatever is going to be in our carts. When we understand that God has it all in control, you can do like I did. Just go with the flow and enjoy the ride and the scenery, being confident all the way!

Jealousy Will Lead You Astray

"For thou shalt worship no other god: for the LORD, whose name is Jealous, is a jealous God."

\-   Exodus 34:14

I have been on a journey in which God has sought to develop me and caused me to "grow up". Oftentimes, this has not been pleasant, but one thing I know is that I am better for it. In fact, we are *always* better for it—each one of us!

There is no human emotion with which God is not in touch or where He will not be able to help us to overcome it. I have felt many strong emotions in my life, but jealousy was one I was not prepared for. In fact, when I speak of confidence above, I can honestly say that jealousy is something that will knock anyone's confidence for six. It's best just to avoid it and be your own person; who really cares what someone else has? We have all that we need, already.

God provides us with this so diligently. So jealously has no place.

It's an ugly emotion that can destroy lives.

I am not a competitive type of person, so I had a really hard time understanding this feeling of jealousy when it showed up. You may find the same, and there is no shame in admitting you feel it, because recognizing and acknowledging it is essential to getting past it.

This is a feeling that brought me to my knees quickly because it was strange and compelling. This feeling is not your friend, so you will need to show it the door as soon as possible; you see, jealousy will cause you to miss what God has in store for you because you will be focused on what others have instead.

Beware, jealousy creeps stealthily into your being when you least expect it, stealing away your time, visions, and dreams. It will make you unfocused, unproductive, bitter and unhappy if you allow it.

Note the latter: I said *if you allow it.*

It's by no means a given that jealousy must consume you. Kick it right out, like the very unwelcome visitor it is.

James 3:14-16 says, "You have bitter jealousy and selfish ambition in your hearts, do not boast and be false to the truth. This is not the wisdom that comes down from above but is earthly, unspiritual, demonic. For where jealousy and selfish ambition exist, there will be disorder and every vile practice."

What this means is that if you allow jealousy to take hold, it will bring other negative and destructive forces into your life, and the more of these you let in, the worse they will become and the harder to get rid. Thinking back to the unwelcome visitor analogy, jealousy will show up at your door, and once it has made itself comfortable on your favorite couch and seen that you are doing nothing about it being there, it will invite all its horrible friends in as well.

So, get it out of your home right away.

You see, Beloved, God has great things in store for you—with your name on them. You need to let Him lead. Let Him decide what is rightfully yours and what will be your own path. Being jealous has no place because it goes against God's will and God's determination.

We often believe we have control over our emotions at first, until they get out of hand and become uncontrollable. Only our God is supposed to be jealous *for us* because he created us, he sees and knows our potential, and he is putting things in place to get us where we are supposed to be spiritual! And again, just as I said about putting the cart before the horse—which God does to ensure you are provided for—so it's similar here. Why be jealous? God will be jealous for you, and you can let Him decide when it's appropriate! Like I said earlier—sit back and enjoy your life's journey because He will look after what needs to be done.

1 Corinthians 3:3-5: "For you are still of the flesh. For while there are jealousy and strife among you, are you not of the flesh and behaving only in a human way?"

1 Corinthians 13:4-8: "Love is patient and kind; love does not envy or boast; it is not arrogant or rude. It does not insist on its own way; it is not irritable or resentful."

Reflecting on God's unique gifts reminds me of a time when my siblings were young.

I brought my brother an expensive toy, and my baby sister four or five "dollar store" type items for Christmas. My brother was very unhappy because he saw the quantity of gifts my sister got and assumed he had been cheated, and that I loved her more. No matter how I explained it, he wouldn't accept it. He didn't care that I had spent more money on him than her; he just couldn't take His eye off of the number of gifts she received versus the single one he had been given.

This behavior begins in early childhood and if we are not careful, can continue into adulthood or suddenly make an ugly appearance when we are down on our luck and someone else seems to be doing better.

The problem here is that not only should we not be making an issue of what others have or have not, but we should not even be comparing ourselves with others around us.

In making comparisons, we are showing human frailty and lacking trust in the Lord to make sensible decisions for each of us. Plus, we should be spiritually generous and enjoy and relish the fact that someone is doing well.

James 4:1-2 says, "What causes quarrels and what causes fights among you? Is it not this that your passions are at war within you? You desire and do not have, so you murder. You covet and cannot obtain, so you fight and quarrel. You do not have, because you do not ask."

Anyway, I learned a precious lesson from this childish rivalry, and the following year, they both got the same quantity of dollar-store gifts. If we are not mature in our thinking, we will present ourselves to God just like my siblings did; while they didn't know any better, it influenced their future gifts, and similarly, we will continue to be unsatisfied with God's provision only because our brother and sister in Christ appear to have more than we do. And being dissatisfied and disgruntled with God's provision is a certain way to become weary, stressed, unhealthy and unpleasant to be around! It is far better for us to trust that our Lord will provide exactly what is right for us.

It's also important to accept that quantity and quality are two separate and distinct concepts. Our Savior knows the difference and how to get you what you need. So, stop looking at everyone else's gifts and start unwrapping your own.

God makes no mistakes, and he alone knows what you need. Sometimes, big gifts come in small packages, and sometimes they come in a trunkful. Either way, be grateful and thankful to God for what you have and what you don't.

Psalm 100:4: "Enter into His gates with thanksgiving and into His courts with praise; give thanks to Him and praise His name."

I have purpose in my heart to love Him, adore Him, cherish Him, and thank Him every chance I get! I will rejoice with you and hope you celebrate with me, understanding we are all drinking water from the same sweet well!

Chapter 2:

Obedience

Samuel said, "Which does the LORD *prefer: obedience or offerings and sacrifices?   It is better to obey him than to sacrifice the best sheep to him.*

- 1 Samuel 15:22

Obedience is the O in C.O.F.F.E.E and it means to be compliant with an order, request, or law, or submission to another's authority. If confidence is our step one, then you can rest assured that obedience is the next logical step. Once we are reliant upon God, we understand the necessity to follow His ways and wisdom.

When I was a young child, my grandmother was famous for telling me, "obedience is better than sacrifice." I never really knew what she meant, but it burned into my consciousness and my soul. I would repeat it often as I entered adulthood, and once I became a believer, her words came to life. I had been conditioned for obedience from an early age and believed I should follow the prescribed path God recommended.

I did not do this perfectly, of course, but I followed the yellow brick road as best as I could.

There is a blessing assigned to obedience. I strongly believe this and have evidenced it on numerous occasions. I often want to go right, despite knowing God is recommending another course. Through trial and error, I now know that His way is blessed, protected, and will work out for my benefit. When we pay heed to the voice of God, it minimizes fear and increases our confidence in our ability to make good decisions; I can trust Him fully with my life and despite what the current circumstances look like, I cannot fail if I follow His voice and leadership.

Isaiah 1:19 reassures us, "if you are willing and obedient, you shall eat the good of the land." And I have found this to be true.

In one of my past positions, the organization had a core value of rigorous obedience to the Constitution. It made me think about my loyalties and what *I* was obedient to.

Many are obedient coffee drinkers and would never miss a day. Many literally do not feel the day has begun until the first cup. No judgement from me, but I encourage you to be that diligent when it comes to the things of God.

What if you refused to start your day until you had communed with God, prayed, or given thanks to the Almighty? What if you knew your energy supply resided in fellowship with Him, instead of your Java? What if you allowed His spirit to wake you and pep you up when you were tired and feeling low? Obedience to Christ provides energy for our souls, providing timely and eternal rewards. I challenge you to spend a moment with God with every cup of coffee you drink for the rest of your life. Obedience will cause you to seek him early in accordance with Scripture.

Proverbs 8:17 tells us, "I love those who love me, and those who seek me early shall find me." As you seek your morning cup, seek God because He promises you will find Him."

Obedience Tip of the Day

Find a quiet place where you can ask yourself the following questions:

When was the last time I said, "yes" to God?

What was I asked to do?

What am I being asked to do now?

Obedience Tip of the Month

Imagine God as a military commander and you as a recruit. What orders have you been given? Use Matthew 10:7-8 as a guide:

"As you go, proclaim this message: 'The Kingdom of Heaven has come near.' Heal the sick, raise the dead, cleanse those who have leprosy, drive out demons. Freely you have received; freely give."

Spend the month diligently preparing a strategy to complete some of the tasks.

Obedience Tip of the Year

Reflect on the following question:

Over the past year, what "good of the land" have I eaten?

***

Are You Coming to the Party or Not?

Let me ask you this question that I have pondered over for many hours.

I was reading the story of the "Prodigal son" found in

Luke 15:11-32 and had a wonderful revelation that I would like to share with the body of believers.

Often, when we read or hear this story, we instantly focus on the younger son and the father. It is a wonderful story of redemption and love that closely mirrors our Heavenly Father's everlasting love towards us. It symbolizes God's willingness to wait patiently for our return and the rejoicing that ensues once we come to our senses and come back home spiritually.

Many times, our story might be related to this parable because, at some point, we were lost in a world of sin and found ourselves associated with the pigs, just as the story implied. We read this story and remember how gracious God has been to us through our failures and periods of rebellion, and usually, we stop there.

I believe this is because we read the Bible through the lens of SELF-GRATIFICATION versus SELF-EXAMINATION.

We often read the Scriptures (if we read them at all) through an enjoyable lens, only looking to reinforce wonderful reminders of what God has done for us versus the lens that says where we are compared to the mirror reflection of Christ.

The often-overlooked character (the older brother) in this parable is relevant to the redeemed believers today seeking self-examination concerning this biblical passage.

As I was reading the parable, my mind started to think of

several prodigal sons I know and how kind God has been to them as I ran down the list of their grievances against God and me (honestly).

At that moment, I began to understand that I suffered from what I call the "older brother syndrome", so I wanted to share this with you in the hopes that you would examine yourself to ensure you also don't suffer from this horrible condition.

Older Brother Syndrome (OBS) is a syndrome that impairs a believer's heart, mind, eyes, ears, mouth, and soul; it is best characterized as the state of being unable to genuinely rejoice with your father—God—when people who might have hurt or caused some form of injuries to you, are returning to the Lord.

It's the inability to look past others' sins because you're too busy looking at all the good you've done, and the failure to fully understand what Jesus did at the cross and not possessing the correct knowledge of the Father's love and redemptive power or authority.

Luke 15:25-27: "Meanwhile, the older son was in the field. When he came near the house, he heard music and dancing. So he called one of the servants and asked him what was going on. 'Your brother has come,' he replied, 'and your father has killed the fattened calf because he has him back safe and sound.'

Syndrome: a group of symptoms that together are characteristic of a specific disorder, disease, or the like. SIN

IS A DISEASE!

Symptoms: Angry, stubborn, arrogant, resentful, disrespectful, ungrateful, boastful, self-absorbed, insecure, bitter, and rude – LORD HAVE MERCY!

Luke 11:28-30: "The older brother became angry and refused to go in. So, His father went out and pleaded with him. But he answered His father, 'Look! All these years I have been slaving for you and never disobeyed your orders. Yet you never gave me even a young goat so I could celebrate with my friends. But when this son of yours who has squandered your property with prostitutes comes home, you kill the fattened calf for him!'"

The danger of OBS is that it causes you to not be satisfied with being a guest at the party; instead, you want to be the guest of honor! It makes one forget that it is the sacrificial blood of Jesus Christ providing you an invite to the party rather than the belief it is your individual works.

You also forget everyone is welcome to run into the arms of the Father, and it is He who determines who is worthy of honor!

You may even be tempted toward disobedience in order to achieve what it is that you desire—so you can get to be in the limelight at the party. Worse still, you see others being disobedient and getting what they asked for, as in Luke 11:28-30, above.

The good news is that there are so many great, effective treatments to cure this syndrome:

Love

1 John 4:20: "Whoever claims to love God yet hates a brother or sister is a liar. For whoever does not love their brother and sister, whom they have seen, cannot love God, whom they have not seen."

1 Peter 4:8: "Above all, love each other deeply because love covers over a multitude of sins."

Renewing your mind

Romans 12:2: "Do not conform to the pattern of this world but be transformed by the renewing of your mind. Then you will be able to test and approve what God's will is—His good, pleasing and perfect will."

Romans 15:5-6: "May the God who gives endurance and encouragement give you the same attitude of mind toward each other that Christ Jesus had, so that with one mind and one voice you may glorify the God and Father of our LORD Jesus Christ."

Seek restoration of your eyes

2 Kings 6:17: "And Elisha prayed, 'Open his eyes, LORD, so that he may see.' Then the LORD opened the servant's eyes, and he looked and saw the hills full of horses and chariots of fire all around Elisha."

Mark 8: 25: "Once more Jesus put His hands on the man's eyes. Then his eyes were opened, his sight was restored, and he saw everything clearly."

The pill of compassion

Exodus 33:19: 'And the LORD said, "I will cause all my goodness to pass in front of you, and I will proclaim my name, the LORD, in your presence. I will have mercy on whom I will have mercy, and I will have compassion on whom I will have compassion."

Romans 9:16: "So then *it is* not of him that willeth, nor of him that runneth, but of God that sheweth mercy."

Dying to self

o Understand you are called to be a servant, not to be served!

o Understand the enemy wants you to be at odds with your fellow brethren and God!

o Understand we are all the dearly beloved of God!

o Understand SELFISHNESS steals your JOY! True JOY is found in Jesus Christ, not in SELF!

Christ's expression of love and acceptance to repentant sinners should comfort you as a believer and as a reassurance of His promises and unconditional love toward us. Still, many believers are being deceived by self-centeredness, clouding our minds from understanding this truth!

Isaiah 49:15: "Can a mother forget the baby at her breast and have no compassion on the child she has borne? Though she may forget, I will not forget you!"

The good news is this syndrome is curable:

1 John 1:9 says, "If we confess our sins, he is faithful and just and will forgive us our sins and purify us from all unrighteousness."

The Bible has made it clear in Luke 15:7: "I tell you that in the same way there will be more rejoicing in heaven over one sinner who repents than over ninety-nine righteous persons who do not need to repent."

As I began to examine what the Lord requires of me, I remember some people who did what many would consider unforgivable against me in the past. At the same time, I have forgiven them, and the Lord has miraculously healed my hurt and pain concerning the situation.

Back then, I felt the Lord telling me, "Toni, I'm throwing a party in their honor because they have returned (repented) unto me, and I love them. Are you coming to the party or are you going to stay outside?" WOW!

Amid the situation, I continue to reflect on all my good, while attempting to balance it against all the wrongs done to me. I must confess it was a turbulent moment in time where I had to check my heart (self-examination) and understand what Christ was trying to teach from this parable of the prodigal son.

I invite you to imagine the person whom you believe to have hurt you the most in your life, now running back into the arms of Christ, seeing Jesus put the saintly robe on them, listening to the party music, and seeing them dancing in their honor. Imagine, everyone is rejoicing, including your Father, and think about how it makes you feel. Before this traumatic reflex, I never wanted to celebrate with those people, and I never thought about the fact that there would be rejoicing in heaven because of their repentance.

And I never thought about my response to this scriptural truth.

Most of us forgive at a distance and try to avoid those who have hurt us deeply, even after we have forgiven. Many believers do not genuinely rejoice at the return of the prodigals to the kingdom; neither do we embrace them with open arms. We stand outside of the party, pouting and waiting for the Father to come and plead with us to "come inside" so we can fill His ears with excuses for our hurts, accusations concerning the honored guest, and a resume of our good works.

I have shared this thought to ask this question, which I've been pondering on for days. "Are you coming to the party or not?"

I have made an irrevocable decision that I will always, by the Lord's grace and strength, get myself ready and in place so I do not miss any party my Heavenly Father throws!

I have an invitation, and no matter who the guest of honor is, I am putting on my dancing shoes, and I am going to REJOICE IN THE LORD!

Are you willing to join me?

Enough

"Enough!" Samuel said to Saul. "Let me tell you what the LORD said to me last night." "Tell me," Saul replied.

- Samuel 15:16

This morning, I was walking and listening to the Bible when the above Scripture seemed to ring out louder than the others.

When I heard the words, "enough", something jumped inside of me. For the past six years, God has literally been providing me with a motto for the upcoming year. The motto for 2020 was, "The year of rock-solid revelations."

Well, I did not know what this meant, and I began the year with great anticipation as I thought God would be revealing deep knowledge. Honestly, I was surprised by how quiet He had been in the beginning of 2020; you see, this book is full of revelations God had given me during the past six years. Every day for five years, God had spoken and carefully filled the pages of my life through His appearance, inspirations, insights, and voice. He spoke into my spirit daily and I assumed 2020 would be no different. Alas, it seemed I was wrong.

What is happening is that God is pulling the training wheels off.

He has been preparing so many of us for such a time as this. How do I know this? Because His silence was a cue for me to act on what He had already said. Several years ago, I found myself in a desert experience; I was in a valley and it was God himself who breathed life back into my dead bones. And now I know He has been refreshing me so I would be able to assist others who would later also find themselves in the desert.

I am a survivor, a conqueror, and a champion for women of God. While I have loved sitting at the feet of Jesus while he mended my broken heart, the time has come for me to help others to heal. Now is the time to share what He has spoken into my heart. Now is the time to pick up our crosses and follow Christ. I am being called to put on the full armor of God and lead others out of the valley of despair, despite the enemies trying to keep us there.

And finally, right now, I feel I can understand it all.

While God promised this year would be full of revelations, I was not exactly expecting the kind or extent of chaos I have experienced and seen. I started writing this devotion before the protests against police brutality began in the United States in response to the death of George Floyd. The verse found in Samuel 15:16 had stopped me in my tracks a week prior, a precursor to what was coming.

In fact, I have been feeling unrest for months, but attributed it to the COVID-19 virus quarantine and the stress of working from home with small children, a stress every mother knows.

But this all pales in comparison to the civil unrest all over the country and for me it solidifies Samuel's assertion. His voice is shouting and reverberating through the halls of

Heaven and it is revelatory to me. Samuels words can be firmly applied to the Body of Christ as God loudly proclaims, "Enough, let me tell you what the Lord said to me last night."

This is causing me to rise, providing me a road map of where my voice goes next.

Little did I know that in a matter of days, George Floyd's death would spark a near civil war in America that continues to unfold. The energy being expended on this issue, both positive and negative, is played out on all social media platforms and in the media. People feel compelled to move, to speak out, to connect with others. Yet, many in the modern church have more passion in justifying their political stances than introducing Christ.

The American church continues to be segregated on Sunday mornings and relatively divided by ideological beliefs. This must end if we are going to be the glorious church without spot or wrinkle that Jesus will come looking for upon His return. Ephesians 5:27 prewarns us concerning the type of church we must look like to catch the Savior's eye. Samuel was simply telling Saul the time for excuses had ended.

Enough, Saul! Stop speaking because the Lord himself has spoken.

In my spirit, I sense this is the season believers have all entered. The time for our excuses concerning why we have not followed God's guidance will no longer be tolerated. Brothers and sisters, we no longer have time to *play* church, we must *be* the church.

There is a generation of lost people in desperate need of the message and truth we have all been taking for granted. We have sat in our beautiful places of worship, complacent, and blessed beyond measure while horrific social atrocities have become commonplace.

We can no longer afford to sit in our churches as if it were meant to be a haven only for believers, while a desperate world is on fire. We have the Living water, the breath of life and the ultimate healer in our midst, yet we no longer share Him with others. Our hearts have grown cold and the light has dimmed for so many in the Body of Christ. We have become disillusioned with the idea that we are followers. The term *sheep* is often used as some measure of slight in our modern culture, yet throughout the New Testament, Jesus refers to us as His sheep. To be a sheep is to be blessed and protected.

This section of my book is all about **O**bedience—the O in C.**O**.F.F.E.E, remember—and Our Father is imploring you to be obedient in this season. He is imploring it now more than ever. And do not look away and pretend it does not apply to you—because he implores it of all of us.

I cannot tell you precisely what it is that He is asking you to do, because it is based on His purpose for your life. I am simply asking you to seek His wisdom and determine what you can do. Some of us will peacefully protest, while some will seek ways to rebuild our communities. I will find ways to help individuals heal, because this is what God has called me to do. I am fully convinced we are living in the last days. This is not a new insight.

I have been hearing the elders say that since I was a little girl, but I see it clearly based upon the condition of the times and actions.

God has provided detailed instructions concerning how His church should respond in times of crises and calm. Rebellion and arrogance are abhorred in the Kingdom of God, yet it seems to be a trademark for our current society and situation. How did we get here? The Bible provides that answer in Genesis 2:17.

God told Adam, "but you must not eat from the tree of the knowledge of good and evil, for when you eat from it, you will certainly die."

It was clear enough, wasn't it?

Yet we find Eve one chapter later not following the instructions the Lord provided. This is exactly King Saul's situation; Samuel relayed God's message to him concerning instructions for the battlefield and what was permissible. Saul deviated, and he modified the word of the Lord to fit his needs and is harshly rebuked when he attempts to explain his actions.

Saul lost his position because he did not follow the Lord's plan. May this never be said of us during these times, and may we earnestly seek God's direction as a member of the Body of Christ and work diligently to fulfill it. May we let go our own agenda and the distractions of the world and carefully walk the collective and individual path Christ prepared for us.

As I watched the breath God had provided to George Floyd leaving his body, I found myself sitting with a deep sorrow once again. I recognized this emotion, this anger, this fear, and this hatred; it was present 2,020 years ago when a man named Jesus's breath left His body at the hands of people who were empowered to maintain law and order. When Jesus died, there was a crowd gathered, some who loved him, some who had shouted, "crucify him" days earlier, and some just casually watching the events of the day as if it were just a pleasant way to pass the time.

This is where we are as a nation and it breaks my heart that we have yet to understand the reason Jesus gave His life. He died for the redemption of all souls because we are equal in importance to Heaven. Jesus used His last breath to state, "it is finished."

He is reverberating Saul's message loud and clear:

"Enough."

"It is finished."

Disobedience was nailed to the cross, recognized as a work of the flesh, hatred was nailed to the cross too, also a work of the flesh. Lastly, murder was illustrated at the cross, but not before the portrait of reconciliation was unveiled. One of Jesus's final earthly acts was to reconcile a sinner to himself, a criminal who hanged next to him, socially distanced, but close enough to obtain eternal connection through the act of spiritual obedience.

No longer can we allow the flesh to divide or prevent the work of the spirit. We can no longer allow political views, ideologies, and identity markers such as race define and impede the mission of the Body of Christ. When you accepted Christ, you were supposed to place those things on the altar to follow Christ. How do I know this? Because Jesus himself said in Matthew 16:24, "deny yourself, pick up your cross and follow me."

Ladies and gentlemen, that is biblical obedience.

If you are going to follow Christ, you will be asked to deny yourself. What part of you is God asking you to deny? I have seen some of the most vicious and hateful rhetoric being circulated from people who claim to follow Christ, concerning racial injustice. As a person who has spent the bulk of her adult life educating people on racial issues and encouraging harmony, I continue to be appalled the most by those who claim Christ, simply because we should be leading the way on this issue with love and, dare I say, modeling forgiveness.

Picking up the cross includes bearing one another's burdens, our literal display of how much we care for humanity. The last step according to Jesus is to follow him. Well, how can you do that when you are being led by every tweet that sparks a fire in your soul?

How can you be led by Christ, if you are listening to

deceptive commentators who only want to distract you from your real goals laid out in Scripture?

How?

How can you?

The world keeps talking about peace as if they do not realize where and how it can be found. I do not blame them for not knowing it is possible, because we have not done a great job of showing them it *is* possible. This should energize you, because there is so much work that each of us can do in this area. Saul became extinct because he placed his own methodology over God's; it was when he began to deviate from the three-step obedience plan that his actions became rebellion.

Let us take heed to this timely narrative and check our intentions, motivations, and direction before we respond. Tensions are high, just as they were for King Saul; however, his inaction caused him to lose favor with God and led to him losing his Kingdom.

This year is coming into view for me, and every day, I am gaining greater understanding of what lies ahead this year. Saints, the Lord is our rock, we must stand on His promises, revelations, and spoken word to be effective in this season. This will require stamina on our part and dedicated effort to shine light into the dark places.

Obedience is a fundamental building block to those who believe in a risen Savior. We rise because He rose. If Jesus is your foundation, it gives you a structure to stand upon as you leverage your energy and gain momentum to spread the gospel. In what areas is God telling you "enough?" In what areas is He no longer willing to listen to your excuses? This is a year of action, but decisive action. Detailed action fully vetted and sanctioned by God, since if we are going to win souls to Christ in this climate and culture, we need wisdom and discernment. We must be fully aligned with the mission and values associated with sharing the Gospel of Jesus Christ.

We have to exercise Ephesians 5:15-16, which states, "Be very careful, then how you live—not as unwise but as wise, making the most of every opportunity, because the days are evil."

You are Going to Lose Some Weight!

Come to me all who are weary and burdened, and I will give you rest.

Take my yoke upon you and learn from me, for I am gentle and humble in heart, and you will find rest for your souls, for my yoke is easy, and my burden is light.

Matthew 11:28-30

Wow, how easily those seven words can grab your attention. At least, that's what happened when they hit my spirit a few months ago. My response was simply, "speak, Lord," and He did; God is always speaking, but it is a matter of us needing to pay heed and listen.

He speaks through nature, people, places, experiences,

and any available medium to get His message to you. I have seen Him show up in some of the most mysterious manners, and I am always looking for him because I know He is everywhere I go.

This perspective has radically changed my life for the better; I now have the excitement I lost in childhood, and every day is an adventure.

To fulfill his request in Matthew 11, the Lord knows we need to lose some weight. When we let go of negative emotions concerning our trials, tribulations, and life's burdens, we begin to lose weight. I am in this process and I can tell you that it isn't easy, but I finally reached a tipping point and realized I must get rid of this excess weight for good.

I am not only referencing physical weight but also, more importantly, spiritual dead weight; in fact, anything that makes it difficult for you to move forward is dead weight. Slimming down is hard work and requires blood, sweat, and tears, but you will not have to do it alone, because it is a group effort. Heaven and Earth share the Lord's blood, your sweat, and tears.

Tears of joy, sorrow, and pain are all possible on your weight loss journey. I have and continue to shed all three, but they have made me better prepared to handle life's difficulties.

As I look around, I see people who, like me, are carrying

all forms of excess weight. Sometimes, it is obvious, but often it is not; now, understand me when I say that I am not talking about whether you are thin or heavy or look happy or sad.

Examine yourself and look *inward,* to know what areas of life could need some working out; this is where you will find all your extra baggage all piled up.

None of us are finished products, and we could all benefit from this self-examination. I am more motivated than ever before to exercise the Word of God because what I observe around me are heavy-laden people. I can hear Jennifer Hudson's voice singing the song, "Heavy, Heavy," from the Dream Girls soundtrack as I think about this.

In life, some walk slowly, some jog, and some make a full sprint as they take their unique journey of life. At what pace are you running your spiritual race? What is keeping you from running better? I do not consider myself a runner, but what I do know from my past running attempts is I pace better when carrying the least amount of weight. As one of God's colorful women, I intend to shine bright and run as long as He allows.

Ladies, do not fall into the trap of discouragement after the first few days of trying. We did not gain this weight overnight, and it will not disappear overnight, but with the words of God ringing in our ears, we can confidently declare to each other, "You are going to lose some weight." This will be accomplished by casting our cares on Him.

Join me as I seek to be able to move faster, feel better, and get healthy to improve my sojourner's experience into the Kingdom of God.

The Color of Christianity is RED

The color of Christianity is RED. In fact, it is blood red, and I hope we all keep that in mind as we journey through our lives. The Body of Christ is the most diverse organization on the planet, united by the same mission, same core values, same motto, same love, and the same leader. It requires each of us to do the same things, provides each of us the same instruction manual, and promises us all an equal opportunity to inherit the same benefits when we are obedient and follow God's manual.

1 John 1:7-9: "But if we walk in the Light, as He is in the Light, we have fellowship one with another, and the blood of Jesus Christ His Son cleanseth us from all sin. If we say that we have no sin, we deceive ourselves, and the truth is not in us. If we confess our sins, he is faithful and just to forgive us our sins and to cleanse us from all unrighteousness."

The truth is an incorruptible source of energy, lifting us and putting us face to face with Jesus, who is our source. He was there from the beginning and will be there in the end. Scripture is clear concerning how we are to walk in the Earth and fellowship with other believers. We are to be known by our love for one another. This is the calling card of Christianity and a sign of our loyalty to the faith we have chosen, yet we continue to allow division to sideline us. We continue to see disagreements amongst those who profess to serve the same God.

I was sharing with my daughter earlier that my existence in life should never trump my Christian living because I am a Christian by definition and description before I am anything else. None of us chose our race, gender, ethnicity, or nationality; God did that, so we have no right to use something God's hand designed to be a barrier or obstacle (imaginary or not) when we serve a God who overcame ALL!

Anyway, I just felt the need to share the color of Christianity is RED. I don't want to offend anyone, but I guess we are all Redskins because if you have accepted the blood of Jesus, red is your new skin color. We can no longer allow shallow issues to divide us in the Kingdom of God, when there are souls at stake.

2 Timothy 2:21-26: "If a man, therefore, purges himself from these, he shall be a vessel unto honor, sanctified, and meet for the master's use, and prepared unto every good work. Flee from youthful lusts: but follow righteousness, faith, charity, peace, with them that call on the Lord out of a pure heart. But foolish and unlearned questions avoid, knowing that they do gender strifes. And the servant of the Lord must not strive; but be gentle unto all men, apt to teach, patient, in meekness instructing those that oppose themselves; if God peradventure will give them repentance to the acknowledging of the truth;

And that they may recover themselves out of the snare of the devil, who are taken captive by him at his will."

I was speaking to my husband on the phone some time ago, and he said: "Hey, there's a cardinal on the back porch." This was my confirmation to share this with you.

So, for those of you who just cannot stomach the thought of embracing the Redskin analogy, you can think of yourself as a beautiful cardinal (red bird) instead.

Chapter 3:

Fervent Prayer

"Do not be slothful in zeal, be fervent in spirit, serve the LORD."

- Romans 12:11

Fervent Prayer is our third letter of C.O.F.F.E.E, and it means to pray fervently, requiring power. And for the believer, this power can be found in many forms, to include the inspired Word of God and the Holy Spirit. I consider the Holy Spirit a power source living inside of us and equivalent to a whole pack of fully charged Energizer batteries!

When we activate our faith in prayer, it is like turning on a light switch. Fervent prayer is intense and full of passion. When we enter the presence of God, we are changed, energized, and renewed. I encourage you to seek God's face early in the day before you get bogged down with the cares of this life.

Our prayers are filling Heaven, like the smell coffee provides in our kitchens and break rooms. Everyone who smells it has anticipation of what comes next. Coffee drinkers everywhere perk up and expect to move from the smell to the taste. I delight in this imagery of knowing God perks up from the pleasant smell of our prayer life and recognizes the aroma, but this always caused me a moment of pause because it also meant He had noticed the stench of my rotten prayer life also.

Prayer is basically talking to God, sincerely and honestly.

Conceptually, we know He already knows what we need and what is bothering us, but prayer should be a regular part of a believer's life. It does not have to be formal or lengthy, but it needs to be authentic. I have not been as diligent in prayer as I should be, as it always seems there are a million other things competing for my time. But I want to encourage you to know Revelations 5:8 prayer is a sweet-smelling aroma in Heaven.

This changed the importance of prayer for me and helped me to understand how vital it is. It is the only contribution of our earthly lives that reaches Heaven and touches God. This is inspiring and should encourage us to reach Heaven with fervor and passion frequently. Just as there are different strengths of coffee, there are different strengths of prayer based on our taste and availability. Consider fervent prayer as a designer coffee brand; it certainly stands out from the off brands and is easily recognized. There is a calmness surrounding those who have believe in the power of persistent prayer, a calmness that would never emanate from any other source.

I am not really a daily coffee drinker, but I recognize the excitement and buzz the aroma causes in coffee enthusiasts.

I have seen the lines at Starbucks, and have known several die-hard coffee drinkers, beginning with my grandmother. I also remember the popular 1980's and 90's Folger's coffee jingle that said, "the best part of waking up is Folger's in your cup."

What if this were true of your prayers? What if the buzz in Heaven was caused by the aroma of our prayers or the lack thereof? What if the jingle is true and the best part of waking up is the spiritual C.O.F.F.E.E in your cup?

I believe it is figuratively true and I hope this book convinces you to fill your cup with a dark, rich roast in order to produce an amazing aroma to draw people to you as you point them towards the cross of Calvary.

Fervent Prayer Tip of the Day

For the next week, purpose to say a prayer before you get out the bed. Even something as short as, "thank you, Lord" can change your daily outlook.

Fervent Prayer Tip of the Month

Create a list of twelve issues or people you need help with (areas of concern, stress, or worry). Assign each one of them to a specific month. During the month, pray about the issue or person. If possible, find a prayer partner you think can help, and also find a Scripture which speaks to the situation and work it into your prayer.

Fervent Prayer Tip of the Year

Make a gratitude list and thank God for at least twelve answered prayers. Write them down somewhere you can reflect on them throughout the years. This would be an excellent reminder for you as you walk with Christ daily, and a legacy of faith to future generations.

***

Consuming Fire

Sometime ago, God gave me a revelation concerning the burns believers encounter when heat/fire are applied to our lives and situations. We all should be vigilant to rid ourselves of the things, thoughts, plans, and people that provoke God's jealousy in our lives.

I bear many scars from painful burns in my life, but God is FAITHFUL to apply the appropriate amount of ointment to each of my blisters, supply/change my bandages and reduce the appearance of scars. JESUS IS THE GOOD PHYSICIAN!

Our co-pays and bills have already been paid, so there's no need to delay making a doctor's appointment! While the tips found for burn care (below) are in the natural sense, I pray God will make it relevant to you in your spiritual walk for you to begin the healing process and reduce the severity of past, current, and future burns. It's no different than when I tell my children to not touch the stove because it's hot….we all know they touch it a few times before they believe what I say. But once they are burned, Mommy is quick to help them recover from the burn, and the same is true for us; some burns are avoidable, and some are not.

No matter how you got burned, the healing process is the same!

Deuteronomy 4:21-24: "There is heat in God's relationship with His people. Within the Ten Commandments, in the second commandment, He says, 'For the LORD your God is a jealous God.'"

What is jealousy? It is a passionate intolerance, even a hostility toward a rival, also defined as vigilance in guarding a possession. In this passage, God is having a passionate reaction against a rival, idolatry. God will not permit idolatry without reacting because idolatry promotes divided loyalties. We are His, and He does not choose to share us with anybody or anything else.

In Deuteronomy 4:24, God's anger becomes so hot that He describes Himself as being a consuming fire. This fire will sometimes touch us as believers and cause varying degrees of burns, but since our God is a healer in all things, I want to share with you the healing process for burn recovery.

Things to Remember When Recovering from Burns:

- Burns are painful experiences that usually leave scars;

- Treat a burn immediately, as left untreated it quickly becomes worse;

- Put burn injury under cold water for several minutes the water prevents it from spreading and getting worse (Jesus is the living water);

- Medicine (Aspirin and ointment) can ease the pain. God's medicine is the WORD, and he applies the individual ointment needed for the situation;

- It is essential to keep the burn clean, even if it is painful to wash it. Wash the burned area gently with water and mild soap. Repeat this cleansing every time you change the bandage.

Isaiah 1:18: "'Come now, let us settle the matter,' says the LORD. 'Though your sins are like scarlet, they shall be as white as snow; though they are red as crimson, they shall be like wool.'"

- Cover the burn with a clean bandage. Change this dressing every day at least once, and after every time it gets wet.

Tips & Warnings

If you believe you have received a large second-degree or third-degree burn, follow Step 1 by running cold water over the affected area. Then seek medical attention. (JESUS - THE GOOD PHYSICIAN).

Note too, it is easy to avoid sunburn, which is usually a first-degree burn, by using a sunblock product with a high sun protection factor (SPF 30 or higher). Be sure to re-apply such a product after getting wet or perspiring a lot.

First degree burns can heal in six days.

Second degree burns can take up to three weeks to heal.

Third-degree burns often take much longer to heal.

- Do not fool around; go to the doctor.
- Do not pop blisters because the infection can occur.
- Do not peel off dead skin.
- Do not peel away clothing that might be stuck to the burn.
- Do not apply butter because it does not help bad burns, and it can cause infection.
- Do not try to heal yourself with homemade remedies!

Trust the Process

On a Friday morning, on the way to school, my daughter asked me, "is cotton smooth?"

I immediately, without hesitation, said, "Yes, in its processed form, not its raw form." Two minutes passed, and in the silence, I began to laugh from my spirit as I realized what God was saying to me. In our original form, we are rarely smooth. We like cotton, have roots (*sin nature*), seeds (*works of flesh*), stems (*attachments*), and a protective outer part boll (*self-preservation*) that cuts if you do not carefully handle or pick it.

At some point in our lives, the Lord processes us (*removes the things that do not look like him or don't benefit the Kingdom*) to make us smooth. OH LORD, HAVE MERCY....

We are being processed by God; he picks us from the cotton fields of life and begins to transform us into a finished product which he intended for us right from the beginning. Just like cotton, we have many ways in which we could be useful.

We can be used in the form of oil, seed, hull, or lint just as cotton for His purpose. We might not know what he wants to make out of our lives, but He does. If so, you are encouraged to stop questioning the process.

Does the cotton seed tell its maker to use the oil instead of the seed? Should the lint be upset it's not hull? Should a cotton sweater be mad it's not cotton pants? God forbid!

You should be glad the Master saw usefulness in us, chose, processed, and turned us into something of value and something fit for His use. Before now, I have resisted the

Master's hand and His process far too long. When He began stripping me away just like the illustration from the cotton plant, I could barely tolerate it. Removing everything not beneficial to the finished product has been challenging and painful, but I am being made beautiful in the process. I am beginning to look like Jesus more and more every day.

Isaiah 48:10: "Behold, I have refined you, but not as silver; I have tried you in the furnace of affliction."

1 Peter 5:10: "And after you have suffered a little while, the God of all grace, who has called you to His eternal glory in Christ, will himself restore, confirm, strengthen, and establish you."

I always knew I was cotton (meaning a natural fiber God harvests), but I have spent a long time trying to: a) process myself (trying to turn myself into the form I thought best):

Jeremiah 29:11: "For I know the plans I have for you, declares the LORD, plans for welfare and not for evil, to give you a future and a hope."

And b) resist the process (refusing to wait for God to reveal my use):

Habakkuk 2:3: "For still the vision awaits its appointed time; it hastens to the end—it will not lie. If it seems slow, wait for it; it will surely come; it will not delay."

The wonderful thing about cotton is that all parts are useful, and many months ago, the Lord encouraged me to "trust the process." Indeed, several people have inspired me with the phrase "the process" and how to endure it. It has been most challenging because I like to be taken through a process simulation from its beginning to finishing stage before I can decide to commit to such a project. When I was in the military, we were often told "trust the process" then, but I asked too many questions.

Some grumpy Sergeant was always telling me, "it'll make sense when you're done."

Well, this is the very same lesson the Lord is trying to teach us. I served over twenty years in the United States military and I never trusted the military process even though it often worked.

After serving God for more than twenty-five years, I have learned I can trust God's process, because I can trust the one in charge of the process! Maybe I just didn't have that same trust in my Sergeant!

Proverbs 3:5-6: "Trust in the LORD with all your heart and do not lean on your own understanding. In all your ways acknowledge Him, and He will make your paths straight."

James 1:4: "But let patience have her perfect work, that ye may be perfect and entire, wanting nothing."

2 Timothy 4:7-9: "I have fought a good fight, I have finished [my] course, I have kept the faith. Henceforth there is laid up for me a crown of righteousness, which the LORD, the righteous judge, shall give me at that day: and not to me only, but unto all them also that love 3 appearing. Do thy diligence to come shortly unto me."

If you struggle with this like I do, I invite you to look in the instruction manual (Bible) and turn to the last page for the picture of the finished product:

Revelation 21:3–5: "And there shall be no more curse: but the throne of God and of the Lamb shall be in it, and his servants shall serve him. And they shall see his face, and his name shall be in their foreheads. And there shall be no night there, and they need no candle, neither light of the sun; for the LORD God giveth them light: and they shall reign for ever and ever."

This is an awesome picture and promise of what lies ahead of us. No matter at what stage you are in the process, you should be grateful to God because you are in His hands. Though the fire can be hot, it is just part of the process. The pain may seem unbearable, but continue to trust the Lord; it's just part of the process. It could be a lonely path, and sometimes stormy, but it is just part of the process; believe me, the process may not be easy, but it is so worth it!

I am a living witness. I have been refined after being tried in a furnace of affliction. God is smoothing all my rough places, and He is taking His time to make me a perfect product ready for His use. Sometimes, I feel like taking charge and rushing through the process. I can only imagine God looking down at me and saying, "I know what I'm doing, trust the process"!

In Matthew 13:31 and 32, Jesus tells the parable of the

mustard seed and gives us insight into trusting God's intended design instead of what we see.

Jesus said, "The kingdom of heaven is like a mustard seed, which a man took and planted in his field. Though it is the smallest of all seeds, yet when it grows, it is the largest of garden plants and becomes a tree, so that the birds come and perch in its branches."

What started out small eventually grew into its intended purpose. This gives me hope, tells me God's process is not hindered by small beginnings or stature. He creates and sustains. The mustard seed is also used in Matthew 17 by Jesus to make a comparison to the believer's faith. Faith is energy in the Kingdom of God, and it can move mountains according to Jesus himself. We need to exercise our faith before, during, and after the process.

Faith causes movement to occur in our souls. Faith has sustained me in harrowing times, and I attempt to pass it on every chance I get by sharing my testimony. We should not be shy about this and should not hesitate to tell people where we get our energy and peace, since they are desperate for solutions and we have the most powerful one in the universe.

It is so amazing not only that we go through a process, but how we go through the process. We can go through it with grace and style or go through it clumsily and chaotically. Honestly, I have experienced both and have discovered in the darkness, God has served as a night light. He is always with me, so there is never really a good reason for me to walk in the dark except I forget to cut the light on.

Often, we will forget the basics when the heat gets turned up, so this is just a reminder to some of us who may need it. No matter how rough the process is, you just remember God is using it to make you smooth. You may be a cotton ball or a cotton sock; that does not matter. What matters is you are completing the process, and once done, you can be utilized by the Master processer (Jesus Christ) to do His will and work.

Psalm 119:105: "Your word is a lamp for my feet, a light on my path"

God's Photo Album

A couple of weeks ago, I was reflecting on so many of my deepest hurts as a new life situation had yet again stirred up unpleasant feelings. As the images began to flash in my mind, the Lord overrode it with a picture.

I saw myself and Jesus smiling. It was a beautiful and fantastic shot, one where it looked like we were having so much fun; my arms were around His shoulders, and we were cheering. It feels so real, but at that moment, I could hear the Lord whispering to me, saying, "that picture is in my photo album."

This knocked me off my feet.

Recently, I have looked inward and revisited all my figurative pictures of myself in comparison to what images would be seen of me in God's photo album. When I think back to the image of Jesus and me, I quickly realize I haven't seen a photo of myself that happy in a very long time, even though I have so many things in my life to make me smile. The Lord had given me a moment in time just like that of Hagar's experience.

Hagar was the Egyptian servant that Sarah permitted Abraham to have a child with. Being a servant could have easily led Hagar to feel invisible, yet the Bible records her experience with God where she realizes her visibility. This must have energized her and helped her to face an uncertain future when she was told to leave Abraham's home with her son.

Genesis 16:13: "She gave this name to the LORD who spoke to her: 'You are the God who sees me,' for she said, 'I have now seen the One who sees me.'"

Whenever I am looking for ways to tap into energy for my soul, I think back on the times God has seen, heard, and valued me in my past. Reliving the goodness of God in my life keeps me energized. It is the equivalent of a black cup of caffeinated coffee: strong, undiluted and keeps me fully awake.

I can look back at my past and remember what God has delivered, done, and promised, using those moments with God to propel me forward. If you need extra energy for the trials you are facing today, write yourself a list of what God has already brought you through and before you know it, you will have convinced yourself that He can bring you through whatever comes next.

If my life had an accompanying photo album, you would find God's hand in every photo. The hand of God has guided, shaped, and protected me. I love to look at my actual old photo albums and reminisce about where I have been and balance it against where I am.

I get lost for hours in looking at my childhood memories and eventually making my way through my children's memories to modern day. When I do this with my focus on God, I gain energy. When I remember what God was doing in my life at that time and the worries I had back then, that are nothing more than memories, I revel in the God I serve.

I get excited from reflecting on what my life was without Christ and what my life is now, and it fires me up. I remember the day I got baptized and how lost I was. I look at my life today and what I have been allowed to accomplish and I am grateful. I want the photos of my life to include God. I want to share my energy with others to help them to heal and move forward to embrace the outstretched hands of God.

I encourage you to stop looking at the photos the enemy has taken and placed in front of you and focus on what is in God's photo album instead.

Someone recently remarked to me that if you think about a photo album, these are all typically pleasant photos. We take pictures to capture things we want to remember, and those are typically happy moments. Sadness will find its way to us in this life, but you don't have to keep staring at the picture. I invite you to focus on what God sees when he looks at you. He sees his beloved son and daughter with Jesus, and it makes God smile. Therefore, the photo God showed me was a picture of Jesus and me because, without him, there is no ME!

Every photo of you and me includes Jesus to make it into the book. I thank God for giving me an image to hold onto when the circumstances of this life look contrary to what I know to be the truth.

Several years ago, I was going through a season of depression; it was hard to focus, and I was sad all the time. I was not my normal self and could not seem to shake it off. Every negative thought the enemy could conjure was sent my way and I was beginning to believe them. One day, I was walking through an office building and on both sides of the walls were photos of employees with captions pertaining to the characteristics they were being rewarded for. There was a picture of a woman with the caption "integrity," and a man with the caption, "honesty."

The whole hallway was lined with these big posters containing what the employee had done and what agency value they exhibited in their work. As I walked down that hallway, I heard God speak to my spirit, "your picture is on my wall."

Tears began to roll down my cheeks as I realized the love and assurance God was pouring out to me. The work I had done for Christ was being considered and judged in Heaven. This moment is branded and seared in my consciousness and serves as one of the reasons I will never doubt Him. In the worst moments of my life, God was there speaking life to me. He never left me alone, and I could always feel His presence. His love for us is unwavering and steady. It has given me the strength to get through dark days and disappointment.

That day changed my perspective concerning how God saw me. I felt like a failure, yet God was reminding me that I belonged to an organization intent on valuing me. I believed God saw my efforts and wanted to inform me that my picture was on His wall. The energy I gained in that moment sustained me through the depressive episode and convinced me I was successful, despite what I was feeling. I wake up successful, because I serve the Living God and because I am a child of God. Whenever anxiety and depression attempt to hold me hostage, I remind myself, "my picture is on God's wall and I am in His photo album."

Because I am a child of God, that makes me a Princess!

I love reminding myself of that fun fact and encourage you to think about your royal lineage as well. Our father is fiercely protective of His children and delights to be good to us. If we remind ourselves of this, we are sure to find a reserve of energy to sustain us for years to come.

I just wanted to share with you that if you are in Christ today, your picture is also in God's photo album, and this image makes me smile whenever I think about it. Remember when you were little, and you would flip through the family album, and something in you jumped when you saw a picture of you. God is saying to us that as His children, something inside of you can jump every day you wake up because there are numerous pictures of you in the best family photo album in existence. I always knew my picture was in my daddy's wallet, but I forgot about the photo album and the wall!

Colossians 3:10: "And have put on the new [man], which is renewed in knowledge after the image of him that created him."

Chapter 4:

Fruit of the Spirit

"I am the true vine, and My Father is the vinedresser. Every branch in Me that does not bear fruit, He takes away; and every branch that bears fruit, He prunes it so that it may bear more fruit. You are already clean because of the word which I have spoken to you."

- John 15:1-8

Fruit of the Spirit is our fourth letter in C.O.F.**F**.E.E.

The fruit of the spirit in the Bible is defined as love, joy, peace, patience, kindness, goodness, faithfulness, gentleness, and self-control. This gives us a frame of reference concerning the attributes God expects to see sprouting from the believer's life. God is watching for our growth and how we bloom. It is our fruit others expect to see, and is what should separate us from non-believers.

Each of these attributes is a direct reflection of who God is, and God's expectation is that those who believe in him should be compelled to reflect him. If you do not see these things manifested in my life right now, I implore you to ask God what He sees.

It is God who created the coffee plant for our pleasure.

Nothing is wasted with the God we serve; nature provides us a plentiful bounty of food and drink. He eloquently provided many fruits and berries for our use. The coffee plant produces coffee berries that when ripe can be picked, processed and dried. Once the process is complete, the beans are roasted and provide the liquid many cannot live without, known as coffee.

Fruits and coffee flavors range from bitter to sweet, just as our lives do. Some prefer bitter coffee, but God makes it clear bitter is not the choice taste for a believer's life.

I can assure you that based upon several stories in the Bible, God expects His trees to yield fruit. When he does not see fruit, he begins to access the value of the tree and its usefulness. I can definitively tell you a few years ago, God stopped by my fig tree of self and cut it down because it was not producing what it was capable of. I had become unproductive in the Kingdom, even though I was serving regularly.

I was reminded of this when I read the parable in Luke 13, which serves as a warning of what happens when the keeper of the vineyard visits and finds nothing to harvest. I believe this is a warning to us. God is expecting to find the fruits of the spirit in each of us. If you honestly believe Jesus is coming soon, it would be prudent to determine what the keeper of the vineyard will find when He stops by and checks in on you.

Fruit of the Spirit Tip of the Day

In the morning, determine what type of fruit you are going to produce today. At the end of the day, assess if you accomplished your goal.

Fruit of the Spirit Tip of the Month

Identify the fruit you struggle with the most. Find Scriptures to support the need for it and purpose this month to determine how you can grow in that area.

Fruit of the Spirit Tip of the Year

Create a fruit of the spirit vision board, listing one fruit for the first nine months of the year. For the last three months, continue to work on the ones you enjoy displaying the most.

***

God's Peacock

The peacock reminds us that we all possess hidden beauty. Last year, I realized this as I watched a peacock at an Amish farmhouse. Peacocks are beautiful, yet it is up to them to decide who gets to see their unique beautiful feathers and when. I believe the same can be said of us. We are all full of potential, yet we're so often afraid to show it. Many of us do not know what God has placed in us for the world to see. As I stood there coaxing this bird to share with me, I began to talk to the bird. I sang to it, talked in a baby voice, and whispered asking it to show me its feathers.

I was only getting a glimpse, but nothing worked. I was at this bird's mercy and on His schedule and somehow, he knew it. It was as if he was saying, "I know you're waiting, but I am not ready."

I patiently waited for this majestic bird to fan out its feathers so I could get a peek. I knew he would display one of my favorite colors and I was determined to see it. As I waited, I couldn't help wondering what God was trying to share with me, because I knew He was speaking, and this was not just another random occasion. This bird and I were locked in a divine occurrence, orchestrated by our creator.

Nature is a wonderful reminder of who our God is and showcases His artwork to include masterpieces. The peacock is in my opinion, a work of art, each one individually designed. Finally, my feathered friend obliged, and if on cue, he strutted past me, made some sound and fanned his feathers. This timely sight was worth the wait. I stood in awe watching his runway moment as I enjoyed our mini photo shoot.

I stayed with him longer than I anticipated, and my daughter asked, "Mom how long are you going to look at the peacock?" If I had been alone, I would have stayed longer because, he was amazing to behold. I began thinking, who is waiting to see my beauty?

When I left, I reflected on the day and realized many of us are like peacocks. We are God's peacocks, because we can fan our feathers when we want to show the world our beauty. We have individual designs and have been hand painted by God, yet many of us are just as stubborn as my feathered friend was. While the world looks on, we hide our gifts and talents until we choose to express them. I thought quietly about the people who need to see our godly works on full display.

How long have they waited? How much longer are we going to make them wait? I want to encourage you to stop hiding. I have decided to be bold, be brave, and be beautiful all year long! Join me; someone is waiting for your beauty.

Do Not be Caught Skinny Dipping

One morning when I woke up, I heard God whispering to me, "Don't be caught skinny dipping!"

I thought it sounded odd, too! Later, God revealed I had been spiritually lost in a sea of hatred! This was a warning from the Lord, and I love to share with you. The Lord began to share that fear makes us naked; it strips us of our protective outer garments. Fear wants you naked because nakedness often gives birth to shame, guilt, and embarrassment. When we begin to feel this way, many of us pull away from God.

2 Timothy 1:7 assures us "God hath not given us the spirit of fear; but of power, and of love, and of a sound mind."

When swimming in any water, it is customary to cover your body and sometimes your head. God was able to give me a clear description of what I needed to survive the waters, how to navigate the waters and how to get out of these waters.

Here's the survival kit God kindly delivered to me.

Survival Kit:

Flotation devices such as a raft, tube, or small lifeboat - Faith

Initially, I had a lifeboat, but my tears due to sorrow quickly flooded my flotation device, and when my faith began to fail, I found myself treading water and afraid.

Bathing suit - Hope and Trust

In the natural, a bathing suit covers the most vulnerable

parts of your body. Spiritually, hope and trust cover the intimate parts of the body also (heart and soul). When you entertain fear, it eats at the fabric of your suit. It begins to tatter, and before you know it, you're naked and completely uncovered.

Swim cap - Redemption

Swim caps are used primarily in pools to protect your hair from chlorine (contaminants), keep your hair out of your face, so it doesn't block your view and enables you to swim faster through the waters. Understanding you have been redeemed by the blood of the Lamb makes it possible to renew your mind daily.

Earplugs - Expectation

If you take too much water into your ears, not only will it prevent you from hearing, but it also leads to infections. Physical and bacterial infections arising from swimming are known as "swimmer's ear". Swimmer's ear can be very painful, annoying, and, ultimately, lead to hearing loss. You must expect to survive, no matter what negativity the enemy says, shouts or whispers. You must protect your ears from the howling of the wind before it infects you.

Goggles – Perseverance

Romans 5:3-5: "More than that, we rejoice in our sufferings, knowing that suffering produces perseverance, and perseverance produces character, and character produces hope, and hope does not put us to shame, because God's love has been poured into our hearts through the Holy Spirit who has been given to us."

We must persevere when faced with suffering in this life. During suffering, our eyes are often clouded with tears and fears, making it hard to see any relief in sight or believe any ships will get close enough to rescue us. We need to look through the lenses of perseverance because these will help us to endure our time in uncomfortable waters.

Flare Gun - Prayer

You must pray while in the waters which seek to devour you. Prayers serve as a clear indicator you want to be rescued and that you can't get yourself out of the waters by yourself.

These prayers let God know your exact location and can be the difference between being lost at sea for a day, a week, or forever.

Freshwater - Truth

It is vital you have access to freshwater during this time. Without water, man does not survive very long. Without the truth of who God is and what he has promised to do for you, you will not last long either.

<u>Navigating the water:</u>

The first thing you need to know if you find yourself in the enemy's waters is that God is in control of all bodies of water, He knows the depth of the waters, the creatures who reside in them, the temperature, the location, and the tide patterns. While most days it feels like I'm drowning, I'm not—because God's ocean of love is never out of my reach.

Survive the raging waters!

The enemy's waters can be described as raging; they are rarely calm! Condemnation tries to drown you, and doubt is the undercurrent attempting to pull us under!

Sharks are present day and night, circling you and even bumping into you to keep you afraid of what your future holds. The raging waters are a mirage or a smokescreen the enemy provides for believers who land in his waters.

The truth is while the waters may be raging, God's waves of peace are crashing over us and will take us safely to shore if we rest in HIM! Jesus specializes in calming the sea, so don't panic!

Swim at your own risk!

Beloved, I implore you not to swim in these dangerous waters! These waters should be marked with a sign declaring, "Swim at your own risk," but the enemy hides the caution sign to trap us.

Take it from me; don't even dip your toe in his waters because before you know it, you will be swept away. Sometimes, we end up in the enemy's waters by choices we usually make in the form of sin. Other times, we end up there for reasons beyond our control. In my case, I didn't choose to swim in the sea of hate willingly; I ended up in these terrible waters due to unresolved anger and fear concerning a very painful situation.

My emotions led me to these waters; they betrayed me! They made me think these waters were safe. I am, however, guilty of testing the waters of the "River of Regret" one too many times during my trials. While attempting to swim in these waters, I have been weary many times.

In my exhaustion, I made two fatal mistakes. First, I began to drink some of the salt water, and second, I lost sight of the shore.

Don't drink salt water!

The saltwater is the equivalent of Satan's lies. This water tricks you into thinking it will satisfy your thirst. We all know saltwater will make you insane before it kills you.

Satan's lies do the same, and when you drink his water, he will decay your mind quickly with negative thoughts and memories of past hurts. The brain is medically the most sensitive organ in the body, and the enemy desires your mind.

He will put images in your mind and distort the situation to make you think it is worse than it is. You will begin to hallucinate that others are against you, and the enemy will isolate you from believers throwing lifelines to you.

If you continue to drink this water, it will lead to death!

Look for the shore!

The shore is a metaphor of the Body of Christ united in

love. Jesus stands on the shore amid believers, teaching us how to live and love like him. The fullness of joy is found on the shore in the form of sand.

Joy is found in every single pebble of sand; it beautifully decorates the shoreline. The shore signals water is near, just as we believers signal to the world that God is near.

And just as the shore glimmers in the sunlight and causes it to be so bright at times, it's blinding, we should reflect the SONLIGHT with a brightness that blinds the enemy and darkness. We should reflect God's glory!

Remember just how many things pull you from the shore.

It was a combination of things that drove me to the deepest parts of the ocean of hate. The pain I experienced from a devastating personal situation left me vulnerable, and I ended up on an emotional roller coaster that dumped me into the ocean of hate. The waters were murky day and night, hungry sea creatures were threatening my life, and I was so thirsty.

During these times, it is critical to look for the shore, seek assistance from the Body of Christ, keep your eyes on the Lord, and make every effort to get back to shore.

Prepare to be rescued:

For those of you with military affiliations, you will find comfort in knowing that God is the entire Department of Defense (DOD)! He is the Army, Navy, Air Force, Marines, and the Coast Guard, while Jesus is the rescue vessel (air, land, or sea) that scours the waters by patrolling and looking for those of us who are lost.

The Holy Spirit is the buoy that guides us in troubled waters. During this experience in the waters, I have clung to the buoy, and I believe it is what has kept me afloat as I awaited rescue.

God is the owner of a fleet of pristine merchant ships, fitted with two large anchors of mercy and grace. He dispatches Jesus to provide us with precious cargo when we refuse to leave the waters and picks us up when we are ready to be rescued. I encourage you to know that even if you are naked and stranded in the middle of the ocean, you *will* be rescued.

Never lose hope or stop trusting God during chaotic waters, or the enemy will catch you skinny dipping and will attempt to overwhelm you.

Hold firm to your faith, be patient while awaiting release from the raging seas of life. In God's waters, there is true freedom.

We are also never without adequate outer garments in God's waters; in fact, we are clothed in His garments of righteousness and holiness made possible only through the finished works of Christ Jesus at the cross of Calvary.

Wisdom is calling with a unique warning "Don't be caught skinny dipping."

Hijacked Peace

I do not know how many of you feel like you are waiting for a "special delivery" from Heaven, but I know I do. I have been desperately seeking peace concerning some personal situations in my life, and no matter how much I kept saying I needed it, I couldn't seem to get it.

I knew God promised His children peace and I could clearly see in Scripture that Jesus was promising me peace repeatedly. Peace is one of the "finished works of Christ" which means that because of His death at the cross, you and I are ensured to have peace as it is readily available; it's a part of our inheritance from His death.

The following Scriptures confirm that Biblical truth….

John 14:27: "Peace I leave with you; my peace I give you. I do not give to you as the world gives. Do not let your hearts be troubled and do not be afraid."

John 16:33: "I have told you these things, so that in me you may have peace. In this world you will have trouble. But take heart! I have overcome the world."

John 20:19: "On the evening of that first day of the week, when the disciples were together, with the doors locked for fear of the Jewish leaders, Jesus came and stood among them and said, 'Peace be with you!'"

John 20:21: "Again Jesus said, 'Peace be with you! As the Father has sent me, I am sending you.'"

Philippians 4:7: "And the peace of God, which

transcends all understanding, will guard your hearts and your minds in Christ Jesus."

Colossians 3:15: "Let the peace of Christ rule in your hearts, since as members of one body you were called to peace. And be thankful."

2 Timothy 1:7: "For the Spirit God gave us does not make us timid, but gives us power, love and self-discipline."

Then it was like a light bulb went off for me yesterday. God gave me a visual illustration of what had happened to my peace; the enemy "hijacked my shipment".

I thought of a FedEx delivery truck being stolen with all the packages still inside. The Bible is clear the enemy comes to STEAL, KILL, and DESTROY!

Follow me, as God sent me peace the day I accepted him as my Lord and personal Savior, and it is available to me every day of my life. I could have signed for the package immediately this week when I asked for it, but because of doubts, fears, and the condition of my heart, I wasn't at home when the driver (Holy Spirit) attempted to deliver my package.

So it went back in the truck for redelivery and then the enemy hijacked the truck with my package of peace still inside.

See, God will not withhold any good thing from His children as he promises in Psalm 84:11: "For the LORD God is a sun and shield; the LORD bestows favor and honor; no good thing does he withhold from those whose walk is blameless."

My walk was not blameless because I had not guarded my heart from FEAR concerning the trouble I am currently facing, and I had begun to walk in fear versus the spirit. So, the next time there is a delay in the good things you are seeking from God, consider the following:

'Is my walk with God blameless?'

Check the condition of your heart *(Troubled or Steady)*

Check the condition of your mouth *(Life versus Death)*

Check the condition of your hands and feet *(Actions)*

Check the condition of your eyes and ears *(Gateways-what you see and hear)*

Check the condition of your mind *(Foundational truths of who God is and what He is willing to do for His people).*

If Yes:

Demand the enemy release your good thing because God is not withholding it, so your shipment must have been hijacked!

We walk in the Authority of Christ and have every right to demand that the enemy take his hands off of our inheritance!

Just because he stole it doesn't mean he won't have to return it and he DOES NOT have the power to destroy or kill what God has given you.

The DEVIL IS A LIAR!

ACCEPT THE PACKAGE!

OPEN IT UP AND WALK IN IT!

GIVE GOD THANKS!

If No:

Ask God to reveal whatever is hindering you from receiving His honor and favor.

Immediately repent!

ACCEPT THE PACKAGE!

OPEN IT UP AND WALK IN IT!

GIVE GOD THANKS!

Brothers and Sisters in Christ, I only share this in order to assist you to be stronger in the Lord! I do not know what the enemy has hijacked from you or what good things are being held up in your life due to the condition of your walk.

All I know is that the Lord does not want you fighting the wind or being distracted by your current trouble. He wants you to rest in His peace while you work on guarding your hearts.

Chapter 5:

Earnest Expectation

The letter E is our fifth letter of C.O.F.F.E.E, and it is Earnest Expectation.

Philippians 1:20 says, "According to my earnest expectation and *my* hope, that in nothing I shall be ashamed, but *that* with all boldness, as always, *so* now also Christ shall be magnified in my body, whether *it be* by life, or by death."

Living with this type of expectation has been a constant source of energy for me. While patience may be a fruit of the spirit, it is not a finished work as far as my Christian walk. I continue to require God's grace and careful instruction in this area. My patience continues to grow over time, but I have mastered the art of expecting good from my Heavenly Father.

He never disappoints and is eager to do good for His children. Over the past few years, I became bold enough to look for birthday gifts from Him. I do not mean physical, materialistic gifts as from a person, but what I call kisses from Heaven. Sometimes, these show up in nature, a song, or a random smile. I have noticed since I expect it, I see it and know He is there.

Expecting God to fulfill His word will reduce anxiety and increase stability. Over time, as God continues to meet your needs, you will trust Him more and more. Such as any relationship we build, we look for consistency, care, and competence. I have never had a need that was not supplied. It was at times delayed or slower than I would have liked, but I always knew I was taken care of. There have been many of my wants that went unfulfilled and I am thankful for His expertise in this area.

I have learned to rest in His loving arms and to bend my will to His word, which is the source of life. His word will never come back void or empty because it is full. Just like the coffee pot of my youth, I have learned to patiently wait for the moment I get to pour out the Lord's provision into a spiritual cup that never runs dry.

Earnest Expectation Tip of the Day

Find a Scripture to accompany a current need. Keep it close to you and read it several times throughout the day. Share it with someone else.

Earnest Expectation Tip of the Month

Reflect on the following questions…What can you expect from God this month? What can He expect from you?

Earnest Expectation Tip of the Year

Select two of your favorite biblical characters, and study all the ways God was trustworthy in their lives. Now compare those elements to what God is currently doing in believers' lives.

***

The Empty Well

"You are a garden fountain, a well of flowing water streaming down from Lebanon."

- Song of Solomon 4:15

My grandmother usually had this proverbial saying (though not from Scripture, but true): *you never miss your water until your well runs dry*!

My thought went back to this as I thought about believers who were clearly in very dry places. In my sentimental view, I often watch or hear some story about yet another man/woman of God who has fallen from grace (human perspective).

I just couldn't understand how someone who claims to be a Christian would willingly behave as if they don't know who God is and what He requires of them. As I asked the Lord for answers, he provided a wonderful illustration that I believe will bless you as you encounter the deserts of this life.

The Lord revealed that those believers had become an "empty well."

A well is used to hold water, and its main purpose is to store water for the time others will need to use it; this could be related to our purpose as believers. Dearly beloved, we are holders of the Living Water (Jesus) so that when we and others need a drink, we have it to give.

It's an easy concept, and most of you are saying, "Yeah, I know that!" But have you considered what happens to believers when their wells run dry? AHH! That's the point of the story!

As we pour out and partake of our well, it is vital that we:

Remain hooked up to the water source, so we continue to have water in our wells:

Personal and corporate time with Jesus (water supplier). **John 4: 14:** "But whosoever drinketh of the water that I shall give him shall be in him a well of water springing up into everlasting life."

Reading the Word, singing songs of praise, trusting in the Lord, acting on our faith and prayer are deposits of water into our own wells.

Repair damage to our wells A.S.A.P:

A small crack can result in significant damage, so fix the leak immediately and rely on God to repair the damage.

Injuries are a natural part of Christian life, but that's no reason to stop providing water even to those who spit it out.

1 Peter 2:24: "He bore our sins in His body on the tree, that we might die to sin and live to righteousness. By His wounds, you have been healed."

<u>Remove contaminants, so our water stays fresh</u>

If there are parasites, bugs, dirt, or anything that does not belong in our wells, we must remove it immediately!

These things may make the water taste bitter to those who are thirsty!

These impurities may also poison those who drink from the well!

James 3:11: "No spring of water pours out sweet water and bitter water from the same opening."

<u>Monitor our water levels:</u>

If we have one drop of the Living Water (Jesus), it's enough, but we should desire to be filled up to the rim of our wells.

Be aware that if no freshwater is flowing into a well, it may not run dry, but it will undoubtedly be stale, which means the water we give and store may not satisfy the people we are giving it to, and they may thirst again!

John 4: 13-14: "Everyone who drinks this water will get thirsty again and again." (Natural water).

If our wells are full of stale water, when they jump into our well, we may overtake them and drown them with stale water if we're no longer watching our mouths and the condition of our hearts.

Psalm 124: 4-5: "Then the waters would have engulfed us, the torrent overwhelmed us; then seething water would have drowned us."

As believers, we often need to be refreshed (restored or maintained by renewing supply) as that's the solution to contaminated water supplies. We are fortunate because we serve a Loving God who specializes in RESTORATION!

2 Corinthians 13:9 (ESV): "For we are glad when we are weak, and you are strong. Your restoration is what we pray for."

What I have realized by the grace of God is that being a shallow well is not ideal, but it's much better than being an empty well because that is one of the most dangerous situations in which a believer can find him or herself for a couple of reasons:

You continue to appear to others as if you have living water flowing through you just because you are a well, and they will keep trying to draw from your well.
You will still pour into other people's and your personal life with SELF and the WORKS OF THE FLESH.
When you are not walking in the SPIRIT, you are walking in the FLESH (Galatians 5).

You infect others and yourself with the gunk that has collected in your tainted water supply.
Revelation 8:11: "The name of the star was Bitter, and a third of the water turned bitter. Many people died because the water was so bitter."

When you are a shallow well versus a deep well, you will begin to thirst yourself, and if you don't get refreshed from your water source, you will eventually die of thirst! As it is in the natural, so is it in the spiritual realm. You are in danger of becoming empty!

2 Samuel 23:15: "David longed for water and said, "Oh, that someone would get me a drink of water from the well near the gate of Bethlehem.""

In your private time, please seek the Lord to determine what your water level is and if you have anything in your well that needs to be removed.

No matter what the answer is, the solution is JESUS!

Psalm 107:35: "He changed deserts into pools of water and dry land into flowing springs."

"God's love is like a waterfall," and **Psalm 42:7** declares, "Deep calls to deep in the roar of your waterfalls."

***

The Weatherman

I have been enjoying the many diverse roles of our Father, that never fail to surprise me.

I recently came upon a thought as I was driving to work when it was overcast, and I was looking at the clouds; I reflected on the fact that "God is the weatherman!"

Think about it; he ultimately controls the weather in our natural and spiritual lives. I wanted to share a few thoughts concerning this revelation briefly. I submit to you that every role of the weatherman is carried out in LOVE. God is genuinely concerned with His work and does it with a Spirit of Excellence.

Since most of us just received our performance evaluations at work, I am reminded that God always gets an "OUTSTANDING" rating for His job as my weatherman.

Below are only a few of the core competencies of our weatherman:

Prepares us for the weather:

Because our God loves us so much, he prepares us for the weather that will come into our lives in the form of rain, storms, strong wind, clouds, thunder, lightning, and hail. This includes hurricanes, floods, tornados, and tsunamis.

Psalm 34:18-20: "The LORD is near to the brokenhearted and saves those who are crushed in spirit. Many are the afflictions of the righteous, But the LORD delivers him out of them all. He keeps all his bones. Not one of them is broken."

John 16:33: "I have told you these things so that in me you may have peace. In this world, you will have trouble. But take heart! I have overcome the world."

In preparation for the weather in our lives, we are provided with several useful items to take with us on our journeys. For you military types, you remember that every member gets standard-issue items that you are responsible for keeping in your "go bag."

The Army of God is no different except your bag is not nearly as heavy compared to all that God has given us.

Rain boots – Mercy and Grace

We each get a constant supply of mercy and grace that will help us weather any storm that may come our way in this life. According to Scripture, His mercy endures forever (Psalm 100:5), so these are not boots off the clearance rack.

Umbrella – Joy

An umbrella provides protection from the discomfort, but it must be opened to be useful. You must also access joy for it to be helpful amid deep sorrow. I am learning that we have to "WILL" ourselves to Joy when we don't feel it.

It is available because the Joy of the Lord is our strength (Nehemiah 8-9). As believers, we know our Joy is found in Jesus, and His face is on your umbrella just like "Doc McStuffins" is on my three year-old's umbrella. It's her favorite, and she can't wait to open it up whether it's raining or not. We should be the same way concerning God's Joy – it will shield us from the cold rain and the hot sun.

Raincoat – Hope

Hope will protect you in all types of weather just as a raincoat protects you.

Romans 5:5: "And hope does not put us to shame, because God's love has been poured out into our hearts through the Holy Spirit, who has been given to us."

Much like a raincoat won't make you look silly when the weather's bad, hope will never make a believer look silly either.

Buttons on the raincoat – Faith

There are levels of faith as one of my brothers in Christ recently explained; there is no faith, little faith, faith, and great faith. I liken this to the buttons on your raincoat. You can have no buttons and your hope will fail because you have no means of keeping the coat on or using it appropriately.

You can have some buttons (little faith), all buttons on the coat fastened (faith) or you can have buttons and Velcro (great faith).

Rain hat – Peace and Velcro on rain hat - Trust

This hat will keep your head dry as the waters pour out of your storm clouds.

Peace can be found in any situation and any circumstance. I know it doesn't feel like it when you're being tossed to and fro, but God's peace surpasses human understanding (Philippians 4:7).

Your trust in God will make it possible for you to walk in peace during the worst storm you've ever experienced. But if you don't have trust, your peace will quickly be lost as the worst part of the storm hits. Trust in God and peace of mind are a compliment to each other.

Knowing that God won't allow you to perish will help

you endure the current weather event.

Creates the weather:

Jonah 1:4: "But the LORD sent out a great wind into the sea, and there was a mighty tempest in the sea so that the ship was like to be broken."

1 Samuel 12:18: "So Samuel called unto the LORD, and the LORD sent thunder and rain that day: and all the people greatly feared the LORD and Samuel."

Cares about the weather:

Mark 4:37-39: "And there arose a fierce gale of wind, and the waves were breaking over the boat so much that the boat was already filling up. Jesus Himself was in the stern, asleep on the cushion; and they woke Him and said to Him, 'Teacher, do You not care that we are perishing?' And He got up and rebuked the wind and said to the sea, 'Hush, be still.' And the wind died down, and it became perfectly calm."

Predicts the weather:

Luke 21:11: "And great earthquakes shall be in divers places, and famines, and pestilences; and fearful sights and great signs shall there be from heaven."

Matthew 24:7: "For nation shall rise against nation, and kingdom against kingdom: and there shall be famines, and pestilences, and earthquakes, in divers places."

Reports the weather:

Matthew 16:2-3: "He answered and said unto them, When it is evening, ye say, [It will be] fair weather: for the sky is red."

Job 37:9: "Out of the south cometh the whirlwind: and cold out of the north."

Protects us from the weather:

Job 1:19: "And, behold, there came a great wind from the wilderness and smote the four corners of the house, and it fell upon the young men, and they are dead, and I only am escaped alone to tell thee."

Nahum 1:3: "The LORD is slow to anger, and great in power, and will not at all acquit [the wicked]: the LORD hath His way in the whirlwind and in the storm, and the clouds are the dust of His feet."

Controls the weather:

1 Kings 8:35-36: "When heaven is shut up, and there is no rain because they have sinned against thee; if they pray toward this place, and confess thy name, and turn from their sin when thou afflictest them. Then hear thou in heaven, and forgive the sin of thy servants, and of thy people Israel, that thou teach them the good way wherein they should walk, and give rain upon thy land, which thou hast given to thy people for an inheritance."

Amos 4:7: "And also I have withholden the rain from

you, when [there were] yet three months to the harvest: and I caused it to rain upon one city, and caused it not to rain upon another city: one piece was rained upon, and the piece whereupon it rained not withered."

Rebuilds after the weather:

Genesis 9:14-16 "Whenever I bring clouds over the earth and the rainbow appears in the clouds, I will remember my covenant between me and you and all living creatures of every kind. Never again will the waters become a flood to destroy all life. Whenever the rainbow appears in the clouds, I will see it and remember the everlasting covenant between God and all living creatures of every kind on the earth.

Brothers and Sisters, I submit to you that God is in control of your life. So often we think we are in control, but I have learned that lesson the hard way. I finally threw my hands up and discovered God had been patiently waiting all this time for me to realize that He was my weatherman. We do have a small role to play in the weather forecasts, but not much more. We can report the weather because we see what is happening around us and others, and we can predict it, meaning Jesus already told us we would have trials and tribulations in this life. So in a sense, we are only repeating what He's told us already—so probably shouldn't take the credit for our predictions!

You may not know when or what kind of weather is coming, but you know it's coming. My grandmother had a way of knowing when bad weather was coming. We too, can often predict what coming based on our thought life, prayer life, love walk or level of faith. I encourage you to get and stay in your lane when it comes to weathering the storms of life. I have been all over the track during my life, running in my path, your path, and the other team's lane. I am firmly planting my feet and attempting to stay in the lane that God designed for me, because though I may stumble, though I may fall, I will get back up and continue the race. We will finish the race because God is coaching, encouraging, and running beside us. Put your trust in him. HE CAN'T, and HE WON'T FAIL YOU! I'm a witness!!

Nahum 1:7 "The LORD is good, a stronghold in the day of trouble; and he knoweth them that trust in him."

Chapter 6:

Everlasting Life

"Verily, verily, I say unto you, He that believeth on me hath everlasting life."

- John 6:47.

Everlasting Life is the final **E** of our morning C.O.F.F.E.**E**! Each morning when I wake, I find a sense of peace and comfort knowing I have a final resting place. For most of my life, I have trusted the fact that Heaven awaits me as home.

I know I have keys to a Kingdom, and I do not doubt this fact. One day, I will open the door to the mansion Jesus has prepared for me. This image and knowledge both give me hope and have provided positive energy that I am delighted to share with others. As a little girl, I began to place my hope in heaven and knew I would one day reside there. It was a childlike hope that grew into a formal commitment to serve the Kings of Kings.

You can garner energy by trusting the promises of God, and one of our greatest promises is everlasting life. Our belief provides us a future home with our Savior. Understanding that Jesus took the form of man and ultimately sacrificed His life on the cross so I could be with Him for eternity is a source of inspiration. It is also motivation to live every day in honor of Him.

If you have accepted Jesus Christ as Lord, you should also know that despite what the conditions of your current life are, there is a place of peace awaiting you. Faith is believing in something you cannot see and while many struggle with this concept, they continue to breathe in air they cannot see either. Yet somehow, they manage to trust this natural phenomenon without fail and instead question the spiritual.

Everlasting life is the sugar in a perfectly satisfying cup of coffee.

Serving Christ through salvation is rewarding within itself, but the promise of eternal life adds to the experience. It gives us hope beyond this one life we live and provides a glimpse of what is to come. Knowing I have an eternal home in a place where tears will be wiped from my eyes, a place of no crying, death, pain, or sorrow can best be described as sweet.

One day, you and I will both enjoy the taste of Heaven and the joys of everlasting life found in the description of Heaven found in Revelation 21:4.

Everlasting Life Tip of the Day

Say to yourself at least twice today, "I am going to live forever."

Everlasting Life Tip of the Month

Remind several that in the Body of Christ, they too are going to live forever.

Everlasting Life Tip of the Year

Set your heart and mind on evangelism, finding creative ways to share Christ far and wide. Think about who will be in heaven because you invited them.

Increase those numbers you can name this year.

***

Switching Seats?

One beautiful morning on the way to school, I was talking to my oldest daughter about "trusting God". I used the side mirrors on the car door to give her an illustration of our trust in Him.

The side mirror on the car is for the driver's benefit mostly, to ensure they have excellent visibility of the road and the objects around them. As an experienced driver, you know one of the first things you do when you get in the car is to check the mirrors and, if needed, adjust them. Well, so do our spiritual side mirrors need adjusting from time to time if we are having trouble seeing God as we drive down the highway of life.

The Purpose of Side Mirrors

The purpose of side mirrors on a car are pretty obvious, but try applying these uses to life:

To see behind you;

To see beside you;

To see your blind spots.

As a driver, I have adjusted my spiritual mirrors daily, trying to see where God was in my situation, and trying to navigate through the traffic and hazards on the road safely.

It seemed that just when my mirrors were perfectly set, someone moved them. When I got in my car the next day, they needed adjusting again.

This happens to all of us in life also; just when we think we have it all together, it all falls apart. It's because we were never intended to be in the driver's seat or to be in charge of the mirrors.

Psalm 46: 1: "God is our refuge and strength, a very present help in trouble."

If we trust God, we know that *He* makes the adjustments as the driver of the vehicle. We believe that He sees all, knows all and is an excellent driver. So, we need not worry about always being in the driving seat because we can find rest when we allow ourselves to be passengers instead of drivers; in fact, the responsibility of being a driver is immense and can be a burden. Ask anyone who's ever been in a car accident or gotten lost.

You, my friend, were designed for the passenger seat, and it's the best place to be.

Any kid will tell you the same; they get to look out the window, take naps, and ask repeatedly, "are we there yet?" because getting to their destination is their only concern. What a liberating way to travel! You should try it sometime soon.

We are children of God, we are riders, and most of us need booster seats, at best. When you get older (mature in your trust level), you'll graduate from the car seat in the back to the passenger seat in the front. But when you don't trust God, you keep the wheel, which means you grab the keys on the way out of the door and hop in the driver's seat every time.

I know this because I've done it all my life, until recently. I love adjusting the mirrors; it made me feel like I was in control. I got to decide where I was going and how much of the road I wanted to see. I didn't realize that I was doing the same thing to God concerning my trust, limiting how much of him I saw in the mirror, until I switched seats. The side mirror gives us a glimpse into how "ever-present" our God really is and why we should trust him fully.

Hebrews 12:2 encourages believers to "fix our eyes on Jesus, the pioneer, and finisher of faith."

As I told my daughter about the side mirror that morning, the passenger mirror safety warning caught my eye; it says, "objects in mirror are closer than they appear." Instantly, I knew God was speaking, and I had missed His message for the whole twenty-six years I'd been driving.

My healing, breakthrough, deliverance, and answers are closer than they appear because God is in the driver's seat. See, when you are in your proper spiritual seat (passenger) this is the mirror you will look at from time to time. You don't have to worry about all the other mirrors the driver has to concern himself with; you can enjoy the view and scenery.

The passenger-side mirror is considered a "convex" mirror because it is used to reflect light outward, not focus it.

Since the mirror forms a virtual image that is inside the mirror, it makes the image look smaller than the object but gets larger as the object approaches the mirror (Wikipedia).

This is a deep revelation, but stick with me. Trusting God is akin to reflecting His light outward; it is knowing that He and all of His promises are closer than they appear.

The "virtual" image is God (often we can't see him), and while His presence may look small, it is much more significant than you could ever imagine. Scripture confirms and explains this phenomenon.

1 Corinthians 13:12: "For now we see indistinctly, as in a mirror, but then face to face; Now I know in part; but then I will know fully, as I am known fully."

Even as a passenger, I have foolishly made God smaller than my problems on occasion. Yet the truth is written on the mirror for all of us to see: "God is near plainly!" The following verses and even science confirm that God is the man in the mirror, and that He is closer than you think.

James 4:8: "Draw near to God, and He will draw near to you. Cleanse your hands, you sinners; and purify your hearts, you double-minded."

Jeremiah 23:23: "Am I a God who is near," declares the LORD, "And not a God far off?"

Psalm 145:18: "The LORD is near to all who call upon Him, to all who call upon Him in truth."

Psalm 73:28: "But as for me, the nearness of God is my

good; I have made the LORD God my refuge, that I may tell of all your works."

Psalm 34:18: "The LORD is near the brokenhearted and saves those who are crushed in spirit." (My personal favorite)

***

Building Your Home on the River of Blessing

I shared in a Bible study some time ago, about how the Lord had taught me a lot about waterways—His rivers, oceans, and even wells. This is an exciting time for me personally as I have a better understanding of the significance of water and how important it is to our Christian walk.

Recently, I was reflecting on making my abode in God's deep rivers of blessing. Many of us instantly equate blessings with money, promotions, jobs, cars, homes, and worldly possessions, but the true blessings are spiritual; the greatest of all is SALVATION!

Can I get an AMEN?

<u>**Blessings**</u> – a favor or gift bestowed by God, thereby bringing happiness, a special favor, mercy, or benefit.

While searching the Scriptures, I found out that there were many rivers of blessing available to us believers such as peace, love, grace, joy, mercy, etc. I believe all of these are fed from the "River of Life" which the Bible describes in Revelation 22:1 "Then the angel showed me the river of the water of life, bright as crystal, flowing from the throne of God and of the Lamb."

As I began to think about this, I could hear the Lord saying, "you want riverfront property, don't you?" I've made it no secret that my ultimate goal in life is to retire to the Caribbean so I can be near the water.

Our God is so good because I don't have to wait to retire; he's already provided me riverfront property. He just wants me to move in. The Scripture describes it as making my *abode* in him. I am convinced the rivers of blessing flow from the Lord (the River of Life), and if I abide in him, I abide in the rivers of blessing right now!

Abode – a home, place where a person resides, residence, dwelling, sojourn, an extended stay in a place.

Abide – dwell, accept without opposition or question, to be conditioned in a particular situation, attitude, relationship.

John 15:7: If you abide in me and my words abide in you, ask what you desire, and it shall be done for you."

This verse sparked a little fire in my soul as I skimmed through it as most of us do; I began to create a list of things I wanted God to do for me. Even though I know better, sometimes I still view Jesus like a genie in a bottle waiting to grant my every wish.

Of course, as I reread it, I realized there are some conditions to be met to get my desires.

1. **If** <u>I abide in Him</u> – This indicates my submission or giving up my will to abide in myself (Toni) versus (Jesus Christ).

   Am I genuinely abiding in him? – OH NO! If I'm honest, I am frequently found abiding in myself. I cringe at the thought of how easily I trust my opinions, thoughts, actions, wants, and desires when balanced against the word of God and the works of Christ.

If yes, move to step 2 – Congratulations!

If no, work on step 1 – Renew your mind and surrender your will.

2. **If** <u>His words abide in</u> me – OH NO! - When the word of God is dwelling in me, it produces a change in me. If His word is in me, this gives me access to ask what I desire and know that I will receive it.

   Are His words abiding in me?

   Although I knew some verses of Scripture, the bigger question is: do my mouth and my feet reflect that His words abide in me?

   This is the part of the Scripture that gave me sober reflection and caused me to REPENT and to make my way right, because if His word truly abides in me, it will flow out of my conversation and lifestyle.

If yes, move to step 3 – Congratulations!

If no, work on step 2 – Read His word and check your mouth.

James 3:10-12: "From the same mouth come both blessing and cursing. My brethren, these things ought not to be this way. Does a fountain send out from the same opening both fresh and bitter water? Can a fig tree, my brethren, produce olives, or a vine produce figs? Nor can salt water produce fresh."

Proverbs 18:21: Death and life *are* in the power of the tongue: and they that love it shall eat the fruit thereof.

3. <u>**Ask** what you desire</u> – This is the good part, but know this – if you abide in Him and His word abides in you; Your earnest desire will be the things that the Lord desires! You won't be longing and praying for worldly things such as boats, mansions, waterfront property, and more toys; instead, you will be thirsty and hunger of spiritual gifts, ministry opportunities, fruits of the spirit, peace for Israel, salvation for unbelievers, and help for hurting people just to name a few

Matthew 7:7: "Ask, and it will be given to you; seek, and you will find; knock, and it will be opened to you. For everyone who asks receives, and he who seeks finds, and to him who knocks it will be opened."

4. <u>**Believe** that it shall be done for you</u> – Know that when your demands (requests) and God's supply (storehouse) align, He can't help but give you what you ask! It's no different than when one of my

children asks me for a hug, and I'm going to give it without thought because what they are asking for aligns with what I want to give them.

Ephesians 1:3: "Praise be to the God and Father of our LORD Jesus Christ, who has blessed us in the heavenly realms with every spiritual blessing in Christ."

I have only shared the lesson God is teaching me to encourage you that our desires for natural pleasures must be balanced against His willingness to give us spiritual pleasures.

While in my natural life, I don't have a waterfront property yet. I just picked up the keys to my brand-new spiritual waterfront property, and I am more than satisfied with the house, the neighborhood, the school district, ease of access to the water, and the views are lovely.

I don't know what your needs are at this moment. All I know is that for me, I need to swim in the river of Joy, Peace, Love, Grace, and Mercy daily. I need the river of Life and Blessing to sustain me as I float, tread, and travel the sometimes chaotic and sometimes calm waters that this life can bring.

I've said all this to say: I'm in the water as we speak, the water feels fine, and the Lord is inviting you to come on in!

When the Birds Continue to Sing

I am concluding this book with a beautiful illustration of a child's positive perspective.

We are currently living amid the 2020 Coronavirus pandemic; panic has been widespread, and life is changing rapidly.

As I was putting my youngest child to bed, I asked him to say his prayers. He said, "God, I pray that everyone in the universe has a great day tomorrow and that the birds are singing tomorrow. He added, "today was great because the birds were singing. I hope they will be singing tomorrow too."

Something about his observation and prayer was simple but profound.

My six-year-old has no reason to fear or panic; he was simply rejoicing in the fact that the birds were singing. This touched my heart in many ways and helped me to refocus in a time where I feel very spastic.

Matthew 10:28 – 29: "Do not be afraid of those who kill the body but cannot kill the soul. Instead, fear the One who can destroy both soul and body in hell. Are not two sparrows sold for a penny? Yet not one of them will fall to the ground apart from the will of your Father."

Birds are referenced numerous times in the Bible, and it has always comforted me to know that God cares ultimately about every creature he created, including us. I do not know what tomorrow will bring, but I know God has already seen it. He is already waiting for me there.

I do not walk in fear, and neither should you. Fear is a natural response to the uncertainty of our times, as FEAR is "False Evidence Appearing Real." But if we stop and keep focused on Jesus, we will find peace. I know many people are seeking normalcy and not finding it. I can only recommend you try to do what my son did, and listen to the birds.

It appears civilization is being given a time-out, which is impressive when I think about how often I was complaining about how busy life had gotten. Now that everything has been put on hold, I find myself unsure of what I should be doing.

I am going to be patient and wait on God for direction.

Psalm 46:10: "Be still, and know that I am God! I will be honored by every nation. I will be honored throughout the world."

Are the birds still singing in your life?

Have you stopped to notice?

If not, find a quiet place and just take an inventory of the sounds you hear. Do you listen to birds at all? I bet you do, and yet many of us never give a thought that the birds are never stressed or worried. They continue to do what God created them to do even when the world around them is falling apart.

The next time you hear a bird singing, see that like a heavenly reminder concerning God's authority, promises, and provision. Anxiety is brought about when we have a lack of trust in God. It is often found in those of us who falsely believe we should be in control. When we realize we are not, our body rejects this notion, and we become anxious. It's a debilitating condition.

I am beginning to understand Jesus's urgency that we turn and become like little children, of which my son reminded me with his prayer and his outlook. In his mind, he always has a reason to see God's goodness. It is that simple; there is no anxiety, no fear, because he knows what direction to look in for certainty. He is young enough to trust fully and not yet old enough to doubt Him.

May we all remember that the way to enter the Kingdom of God is to receive it like a child.

Reflections

As we approach the end of this book, I want to leave you with a short, final reminder of C.O.F.F.E.E—what it stands for, and how you can remember it and use it in daily life.

Confidence:

For the past six years, God has provided a personal theme for me to think upon. 2020 is the year of Rock-Solid Revelations, hence God is graciously bringing that to pass through this work…Amen! This gesture has given me great confidence that God has provided a path for me to follow!

Obedience:

I have spent most of my life planning and then attempting to control my own life.

Even though I was a believer, I never fully surrendered control until I had problems I could not solve, and I rarely asked God for His constant guidance because I believed I knew best. Well, let me tell you, this is pride and—just as in the popular saying—it comes before the fall.

After I fell hard a few years ago, I learned to ask for His daily direction. I have not always wanted to follow the advice, but I have done so out of obedience.

I find comfort in knowing I am on His side and honoring him through obedience. I would not be honest if I said this was always easy, but I know God knows what is best for me.

Fervent Prayer:

My prayers of fervency are symbolized by the times I cried out in desperation, when I felt God's presence, power, and persistent love. It was a force, lifting my mood and spirit. It is humbling when I think back to those times and how I felt in the moment.

They have mostly been reserved for times of trouble and intense suffering.

During the good times, I am typically guilty of rendering those short, silent quick prayers. In trying times, my prayers were raw, yet filled with an unwavering faith. I have been diligently working toward making every morning consist of regular time spent communing with God.

__Fruit of the Spirit:__

Several of the fruits come naturally to me, such as joy, gentleness, and kindness. I was taught those attributes in childhood. I modeled them after many of my family members, and what I didn't learn about self-control and faithfulness from my family was quickly instilled by the military.

But the one fruit of the spirit which keeps me awake at night is love.

Many years ago, one Scripture kept tugging at my heart concerning the way God expects us to love. 1 Corinthians 13:2 continues to challenge me and helps me to understand the heavenly hierarchy between faith and love. Faith was not the issue for me, but love was, and it was made painfully clear that without love, I am nothing.

I have set a goal to learn to love the way God requires and I work on it every day.

__Earnest Expectation:__

Like any good parent, we can look at God as a Father. One of His many names is Abba, a term of endearment and referring to God as a daddy. Like little children, we can trust and rely on our "Daddy God."

I am a huge Avengers movie fan, so the notion of superheroes has always caught my attention. This concept is not new though, since the Old Testament refers to God as an avenger. So, God is the original Avenger. He will fight for you, defend you, and protect you from your enemies.

I could fill another book with the numerous times he stopped death and saved my life. I can recall many issues and enemies that caused me sleepless nights that no longer matter. God protected me, and now I expect He will do it again in the future.

Everlasting Life:

One night, I dreamed I was in Heaven; I was in an exceptionally beautiful building and Jesus was teaching. I never looked up because of my shame. I did not feel worthy, but Jesus invited me to get up and kept motioning me to stand. I was on my knees the entire time and would not look up.

When I woke up, I marveled at how beautiful the floors were. This was over ten years ago, but I remembered two things. First, Jesus appeared frustrated with my inability to recognize His death made me worthy. I imagine it must be disappointing when He tells us to rise and we allow shame, guilt and sin to keep us on our knees. One day, I will enter the beautiful building again and I will be confident enough to check out the rest of the room, standing tall beside my King.

Conclusion

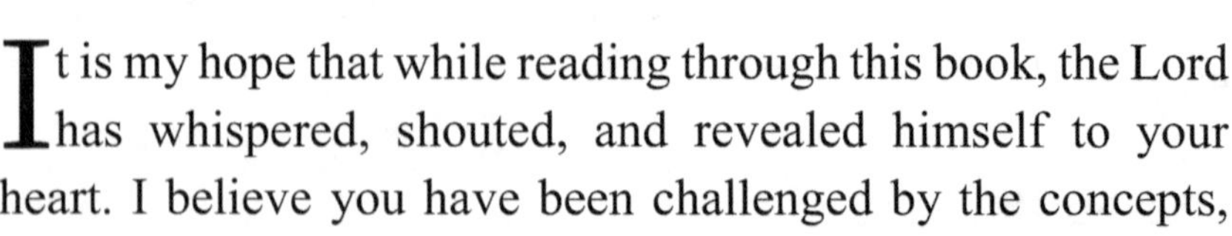

It is my hope that while reading through this book, the Lord has whispered, shouted, and revealed himself to your heart. I believe you have been challenged by the concepts, questions, and wonderings toward which you have been pointed.

My refuge has been found in the consistent belief that I am loved and able to move mountains because of the shed blood of Jesus Christ.

There was a time in my life when this belief was based on my grandmother's faith, but these days, I am mature and experienced enough to know my faith is rooted in my own beliefs, believing Jesus died on the cross in accordance with biblical theology for my sins. I will forever point people in the direction of the cross because it is where our lives begin. One day, while sitting in a Bible study session, a brother in Christ passionately declared, "it's the Cross or nothing!"

It pierced my soul when he said it because it is the truth. I have no other proven source or direction to offer; it is where I find healing, heritage, and hope.

The cross is where I gained a forever home. I will always be dependent upon heaven, its inhabitants, and my Savior. I see God as a Father, Jesus as a brother, and the Holy Spirit as a comforter. They all have served as faithful teachers, guiding me daily as I seek to live a life that shines bright. I realize some of you reading this book may not believe in God but were willing to open your souls in your pursuit of energy.

I want to thank you, and what I have come to realize is that even when we do not believe in God, He continues to believe in us.

He knows what the plan for your life is and wants to share it with you.

If you found areas or concepts that caused you concern, do not worry. Rejoice and turn to God. Seek him first for understanding, pray for wisdom, repent if needed, and move forward. If you have never asked Jesus to be your Lord and personal savior, why not do it right now? You can do it no matter where you are reading this book.

You could be on an airplane or in your bedroom; God is already there, always available. I gave my life to God in Air Force basic training because I was desperate for the peace He promised, so if you too want permanent energy for your soul, try Jesus. If you are seeking a relationship with Jesus, you can simply confess with your mouth the Lord Jesus and believe in your heart that God raised Him from the dead, and you will be saved.

I offer a simple prayer for any of you who want to join

the Body of Christ:

Jesus, I believe you died on the cross for my sins. Though they are many, you had the energy to rise again from the dead in order that I might be forgiven. Take this life and do with it what you will. Thank you!

This simple confession will change your life. In Christ, we can overcome whatever troubles we encounter, we can be calm in raging waters, and we can rest in dynamic chaos.

Our loving Father looks on, inviting us to the party of a lifetime, and one day, I hope to see you there. But in the meantime, always start your day with C.O.F.F.E.E.

Your Sister in Christ,

T. Pearl Joynz

C.O.F.F.E.E
Tips of a Lifetime

Confidence Tip of a Lifetime:

Write a resume for God, and make it personal by listing what He has done in your life. List the job titles He's held, the duties, and then reflect on the salary you have provided for all the work He has done for you. This is a humbling experience and exercise, but it serves as a reminder that He is the best person for every job, and it will build your confidence in Him to see what He has already done.

Obedience Tip of a Lifetime:

Write an obedience resume for yourself. Your job is to be an obedient follower of Christ. What can you list? What have you done? What are you striving toward accomplishing? What special skills do you have as it relates to obedience?

Fervent Prayer Tip of a Lifetime:

Find a consistent place to seek God in prayer on a regular basis. It could be a prayer closet, in your car, someplace outdoors or anywhere you feel connected to His spirit. During this time, imagine what picture God has of you in His photo album.

<u>Fruit of the Spirit Tip of a Lifetime:</u>

Research stories of people of faith who used the same fruit of the spirit you want to develop. Throughout the year, watch movies, read books, etc. to discover practical tips to stimulate your growth.

<u>Earnest Expectation Tip of a Lifetime:</u>

Make a list of the things you now have that you were once waiting for. Make a list of what you are *still* waiting for. Realizing what God has done for you in the past will serve as a reminder of what He can do in your future.

<u>Everlasting Life Tip of a Lifetime:</u>

Design your dream house, find a picture or blueprints. Imagine—if you could build any house—what it would look like, where it would be located and what would surround it.

Author's Bio

T. Pearl Joynz (Toni) is a daughter of God first and foremost, which technically makes her a princess. She accepted Christ at the age of nineteen and never looked back. She has a heart of worship, and hands and feet of praise.

She is a gifted leader, teacher, speaker, poet, dancer, published writer and a Champion for Women of God. She retired from the U.S. Air Force in 2014 after serving twenty-one years, and is a former Christian radio show host, and a sought-after speaker. Toni completed her Ph.D. in Education in 2017 because God assured her, He was going to use it for His glory.

Nothing she has learned or experienced in the natural compares with what she has been taught and experienced in the Spirit. Her greatest life lesson has been that our love for God is no match for God's love for us.

One of T. Pearl Joynz's favorite Scriptures is 2 Corinthians 5:13:

"If we are "out of our mind," as some say, it is for God; if we are in our right mind, it is for you."

Mrs. Joynz aspires to share a simple message with the

bitter, broken, and betrayed:

"Time alone does not heal all wounds, but God can!"

9 781735 206301